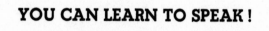

YOU CAN LEARN TO SPEAK !

You Can Learn To Speak!

BY

ROYAL L. GARFF, PH. D.

Professor of Speech and Marketing
University of Utah

Introduction by Earl Nightingale

Illustrated by Dave Burton

Special Revised Edition published by
THE BOND WHEELWRIGHT COMPANY
Porter's Landing, Freeport, Maine, 04032

Library Catalogue card number — 51-7815

First M.I.A. printing, June, 1950
Second printing, September, 1950
Third printing, May, 1951
Fourth printing, June, 1952
Fifth printing, June, 1952
Sixth printing, May, 1954
Seventh printing, June, 1954
Eighth printing, June, 1956
Ninth printing, June, 1959
Tenth printing, April, 1962
Eleventh printing, June, 1962
Twelfth printing, June, 1962
Thirteenth printing, June, 1964
Fourteenth printing, June, 1964
Fifteenth printing, October, 1965
(Revised edition)
Sixteenth printing, January, 1966

Lithographed in the United States of America by
WHEELWRIGHT LITHOGRAPHING COMPANY
975 South West Temple
Salt Lake City, Utah 84101

CONTENTS

The Author: Dr. Royal L. Garff

Introduction by Earl Nightingale

INTRODUCTION

by Earl Nightingale

Never in the history of man has spoken communication been so vital. That we live in a world of speech is obvious — we speak to men in outer space, we speak to friend and foe at the United Nations, the Catholic Mass is spoken and sung in English, to give but a few examples. Equally obvious is the fact that we can't all be astronauts, statesmen, or church leaders. But we all do have, in our own spheres, a message to give to one or more persons. Perhaps to a local improvement committee, the PTA, a church club, lodge group or politcal rally . . . a sales or management meeting, a labor group . . . you name it. Whatever it may be, read this book with your personal speech challenge in mind.

Some years back, when a nationally-known sports announcer met an untimely death in an auto accident, many people were amazed to learn that this brilliantly vocal man had once been the victim of a very serious speech impediment. Like Demosthenes, he had labored in secret to overcome his affliction and had prevailed.

Another friend of mine was for many years a plant manager for one of the country's largest and best known food processors. His had been a small plant, but he had managed it well and profitably for the parent company and at last his time came to move up. He was selected by top management to head one of the company's largest plants. It was a wonderful promotion including a substantial raise in pay. Additionally, it placed him in direct line for ultimate promotion to the inner circle itself — the very top management.

His promotion was to be announced at a large company banquet. In attendance would be all the management people of the company, including the plant managers from all over the country, and their wives. The president was to make his annual speech, ending it with the good news of my friend's promotion. It was naturally expected that my friend would make an acceptance speech.

Two weeks before the event, my friend called on me. He confessed that the thought of making a speech to so august a gathering terrified him. We had a long talk. I pointed out to him that his speech need not be a long one. In fact, it would be best if he kept it quite short. I then showed him how I outline a speech — how I use a few notes to keep me on course — and I loaned him some material I felt would be helpful.

Later, I learned from a third person what happened on the night of of the banquet. It seems my friend was in such a sweat about having to stand on his feet and give even a short speech (and those of us who are called upon to talk know what stomach-wrenching near-panic this can cause), he had fortified himself at the bar before dinner. He was not much of a drinker as a rule, and since one martini seemed to bolster his courage, he had two. This so encouraged him, he had a third. He then found himself actually looking forward to speaking. He even felt that he could now adlib his speech and dispense with his notes. While he was at it . . . he thought it might be a good time to get some things off his chest that had been bothering him for some time regarding company policy. Thus encouraged, he had a fourth martini.

An hour later, the president made the announcement as to the man selected to manage the new big plant. All eyes turned to my friend and his wife who were seated at the speakers' table. Slowly . . . using the table to steady him, my friend managed to get to his feet. He started to turn to make his way to the lectern, but there were simply too many legs of chairs. A terrible silence fell over the room as he fell. Helping hands raised him to his feet and to the lectern . . . but he was too far gone. He could only mumble incoherently.

Needless to say . . . instead of the promotion, he was instantly relegated to company limbo. His fear of giving even a short acceptance speech had ruined his future with the company. Nor did it do anything to help his marriage.

I have chosen, obviously, two extreme examples. The one who not only overcame his stage fright — which comes naturally to virtually everyone — but who went on to wealth and fame by overcoming a serious speech impediment. The other, with no impediment, who was an excellent manager and did deserve the promotion, but who ruined it all because of his fear of public speaking.

Speaking effectively is certainly one of the most valuable achievements of life. And it is exactly that — an achievement. It is learned . . . whether by Demosthenes or Churchill. And it is more than a coincidence that those who learn this art well have a way of arriving at or close to the top in whatever line they pursue.

In order to learn to speak confidently and well, you could not, in my opinion, have found a book better able to help you than this one.

You may never be called upon to stand up and speak before a large gathering. And then, again, you might. But we communicate with others every day with the spoken word. Our spoken communication should be interesting, vital, colorful and, above all, effective. That this book helps us substantially in this regard is testified to by the fact that this introduction is for its sixteenth printing.

You will become a far more effective communicator if you will make the contents of this excellent book a part of your knowledge.

EARL NIGHTINGALE
Chicago, Illinois   1966

CHAPTER I

SPEAK UP AND BE SOMEBODY

AN ARAB CHIEF tells the story* of a spy who had been captured and sentenced to death by a general of the Persian army. The general had fallen upon a strange and weird custom. He permitted the condemned person to make a choice. He could either face the firing squad or pass through the Black Door.

As the moment of execution drew near, the general ordered the spy to be brought before him for a short, final interview, the primary purpose of which was to receive the answer of the doomed man to the query: "Which shall it be — the firing squad or the Black Door?"

This was not an easy question, and the prisoner hesitated, but soon made it known that he much preferred the firing squad. Not long thereafter a volley of shots in the courtyard announced that the grim sentence had been fulfilled.

The general, staring at his boots, turned to his aide and said, "You see how it is with men; they will always

---

* Origin of the story is unknown. It was related in the writer's speech class by a student.

prefer the known way to the unknown. It is characteristic of people to be afraid of the undefined. And yet I gave him his choice."

"What lies beyond the Black Door?" asked the aide.

"Freedom," replied the general, "and I've known only a few men brave enough to take it."

Open the Door

Perhaps this impresses you as a fantastic story, but it dramatizes a truth: *fear of the unknown stops people from liberating themselves!*

Witness the spectacle of a hotel manager pacing up and down in front of an office building with indecision furrowed on his brow. Upstairs are a number of prominent men of the community learning the art of public speaking.

This executive held membership in the group. He paid his tuition for the privilege. He needed the training. In fact, his position depended upon it, because his failure to express himself well seriously dampened the *esprit de corps* of those who depended upon him for leadership.

His steps wavered at the entrance because he was afraid to risk his sensitive pride while seeking the help he so desperately needed. He could not make up his mind to go through the door.

Men and women everywhere are confronted with a comparable problem and are shrinking from its solution. They do not seem to realize that speaking, like walking or eating, is a normal function and involves no crisis. The training recommended in this volume is intended to help you open the door to greater speech power.

SPEECH TO BE MADE		YOUR ATTITUDE
I DID	100	ACCOMPLISHMENT
I WILL	90	DETERMINATION
I CAN	80	KNOWLEDGE OF POWER
I WILL TRY	70	WILLINGNESS
I THINK I CAN	60	FAITH IN SELF
DO YOU THINK I CAN ?	50	LACK OF CONFIDENCE
I WISH I COULD	40	DESIRE
I CAN'T	30	INABILITY
I DON'T CARE	20	INDIFFERENCE
I DON'T WANT TO	10	NO DESIRE
I WON'T	0	STUBBORNNESS

* Copyright by Rex McKean. Reprinted by permission.

The Myth of the Born Speaker

It is folly to regard anyone as a born speaker. History demonstrates that few, if any, of those who attain oratorical greatness are distinguished because of natural gifts alone. ✓Teachers know that too often the best endowed students achieve less than those of inferior talents. The reason is simple. A person who overrates his natural capacity is handicapped at the outset by a lavish opinion of himself. What heredity gives to a person is secondary to training and preparation. The assertion, "Either you are a born speaker or you are not" is foolishness!

Every Round Goes Higher, Higher

No person has appeared before an audience with effectiveness until he has said to himself: "I think I can," "I will try," "I can," "I will," and "I did!" These expressions indicate faith in self, willingness, knowledge, determination, and accomplishment.

To climb the heights of speaking achievement, just keep on trying and learning until there is born in your heart an absolute conviction that *you can speak,* and then there is nothing in the world that can stop you!

Demosthenes Still Speaks

You may recall the story of Demosthenes.* He was born with a weak voice; he lisped, enunciated poorly, and mispronounced the letter "r." You probably remember how determination helped him overcome his handicaps. He practiced with pebbles in his mouth, shouted over

---

* See A. W. Packard, *Demosthenes,* pp. 28-30. G. P. Putnam's Sons. New York. 1914.

the roaring breakers on the shores of Phaleron, recited while running uphill striving to deliver more and more lines with one breath, and rehearsed before a mirror to correct his gestures.

But do you know that in spite of all this heroic effort he failed more than once to win his listeners, and that his utterance was met with raucous laughter? Do you know that he built an underground chamber where he could project his voice and perfect his delivery without interruption? And do you know that for three months at a time he shaved only one side of his head so that he would resist the temptation to desert his training program and mingle with his fellows in pleasurable pursuits?

Notwithstanding many obstacles, Demosthenes became one of the world's great orators. He showed absolute contempt for his own shortcomings. He was one of those heroic souls who push their way through doors draped black with discouragement.

Do the Thing

You may assume that only a Demosthenes could energize such a program of self-discipline, but Dorothea Brande* asserts: "Failure indicates that energy has been poured into the wrong channel. *It takes energy to fail* . . . . 'Do not act

---

* *Wake Up and Live*, pp. 15, 34, 80, 85, 91. Simon and Schuster, New York. 1936. Reprinted by permission.

as if you had a thousand years to live,' Marcus Aurelius warned himself in his maxims. All those in the grip of the Will to Fail act as if they had a thousand years before them. Whether they dream or dance, they spend their precious hours as though the store of them were inexhaustible . . . .

"As Dorothy Canfield Fisher says in her excellent little book for parents and teachers, *Self-Reliance,* 'Success or failure in adult life depends largely on the energy, courage, and self-reliance with which one attacks the problem of making his dreams come true. Self-confidence in any enterprise comes as a rule from remembrance of past success.'

"In everyday life, then, if you are ineffectual in your daily encounters and unproductive in your work, you are to that extent acting *as if* you willed to fail. Turn that attitude inside out, consciously decide that your 'As If' shall be healthy and vital, shall be aimed towards accomplishment, and you have made success a truth for yourself.

" 'The law of nature is: Do the thing and you shall have the power; but they who do not do the thing have not the power.'

"*Act as if it were impossible to fail.*"

Keep Aspirations Alive

Let it not be with your aspirations as Heywood Broun felt it was with his college mates in deciding not to attend a class reunion. He said: " 'The reason I'm not going is that I don't like to eat with dead men.' Twenty years before, a class of college boys had faced the future 'strong in will to strive, to seek, to find, and not to yield.' But in many instances the bright will and the bright dream had lacked the vitality to live. They had quietly died, and in their place had come earthbound complacency. Heywood Broun knew what had happened. He could not make merry at the banquet table where he would have to look at lives that were the graveyards of high expectations."*

If you possess the courage to undertake speech training, will you continue to make the effort? Will you take advantage of each opportunity to speak? Will you prepare each assignment? There is no end to the doors which may confront you. Be encouraged by the new strength, and new skills, and a stronger will to move on through the next.

Rewards Worth the Price

Weigh the appraisal of a former vice-president of Montgomery Ward and Company. He writes about one hundred young men in his organization who studied public speaking. "What happened to the young men who took the classes in speech training? When they came with us they averaged on a par with hundreds of others engaged at the same time. They had about the same educational advantages and were selected to meet the same personnel standards . . . . I am thoroughly convinced that their increased measure of progress is due entirely to the fact that they learned to become articulate about their work and their ideas. I have seen a great many of them present material, catalogue plans, layouts and promotional programs to management groups. I have watched them speak with continually increasing vigor and clarity to a point where senior officers of the company have singled them out for advancement."†

---

* Nat G. Long in *Pulpit Preaching*.
† From a letter to the author.

An examination of their records showed that within a few years sixty percent of these young men occupied key positions with the firm and that twenty percent held key positions with other companies. Nearly all of the plus-ability that put these young men ahead of their fellows was acquired through tenacious effort and study.

The Rule of the People

Walt Whitman wrote, "I hear America singing!" He could just as poetically have exclaimed, "I hear America speaking!" The following montage indicates how varied are the activities in which all of us speak, and how right it is that we be heard:

"Talk founded the Union, nurtured it, and preserved it . . . .

"Talk is our daily fare —

"The white-bosomed lecturer regaling the Tuesday Ladies' Club, the prisoner at the bar testifying in his own behalf, the editorial writer complaining of civic abuses;

"The actor declaiming behind the footlights, the movie star speaking on the screen, the librarian dispensing the accumulated talk of ages, the professor holding forth to his students;

"The debating society, the meeting of the aldermen, the minister in the pulpit, the traveler in the lounge car, the soap-box orator with his flag and his bundle of epigrams;

"The opinions of the solemn magistrate and . . . .

"The opinions of the animated mouse — Words, ideas, in a never-ending stream, from the enduring wisdom of the great and the good to the puniest thought troubling the feeblest brain.

"All are listened to, all add up to something and we call it the *rule of the people*, the people who are *free to say the words*."*

Speak As Free Men

In response to the privilege of free speech too often the businessman makes his hollow apologies, and the club woman recites her platitudinous explanations. The church member too often utters trite statements about his shortcomings and relies too meagerly upon his own preparation and too heavily upon the inspiration of the moment.

Freedom of speech does not grant us the right to shout, "Fire," in a crowded theatre, cautioned Justice Holmes, but it is the foundation of our democratic life.

"If men cannot reach each other, they certainly cannot understand one another. Like savages, they may make signs and noises, but . . . only a clear word, spoken in good time, serves as a touchstone of the mind."†

In his highest moment, the great speaker is activated with aggressive conviction, and he pronounces his conclusion as ultimate truth. He speaks *as one having authority* and, therefore, *the common people hear him gladly*.

All this means that if you are to speak up and be somebody, you must *open the door, have something to say,* and *know how to say it !*

---

* "The Four Freedoms," by Office of War Information, in *Bulletin of the American Association of University Professors*, Volume XXVIII, Number 4, p. 442.

† *Argonaut*, May 13, 1949, inside front cover.

CHAPTER II

WHY FEAR ? — BE OF GOOD CHEER !

> The centipede was happy quite
> Until the frog for fun
> Said, "Pray which leg comes after which?"
> Which wrought his mind to such a pitch
> He lay distracted in the ditch,
> Considering how to run.

These lines describe the feelings of the self-conscious speaker who stands befuddled before an audience. When  he thinks of making a speech, the problem of "which comes after which" begins to tighten his verbal legs. Then, like the centipede, his mind is "wrought to such a pitch, he lay distracted in the ditch."

Adeline Reynolds, outstanding success as the director of her own business school, has expressed a fundamental truth that applies to the speaker. She said proudly: "In a year, businessmen were paying extra to get my students. I didn't just teach them typing and shorthand. I trained them not to be afraid, because a fearful heart always bungles."*

Weeds of Fear

The importance of overcoming any kind of fear is described by Dr. Irving S. Cutter, late Dean of Northwestern University's Medical School: "If some good fairy should come along and grant the power to cure one single

---

* Dorothy Walworth, "The Heart That Did Not Break," in *Reader's Digest*, December 1949, p. 38. Reprinted by permission.

disease, perhaps most of us would choose the ability to destroy cancer; to wipe it from the face of the earth. On second thought, I am not sure but that I would choose mastery over worry, because I am convinced that with the mind at ease, with thoughts substantially at peace, all our vital organs would function far more efficiently.

"While we can look upon this tendency to worry as due to disposition, fundamentally it is a child of fear. No matter how intelligent the individual may be — if the habit of crossing bridges before they are even approached is deeply rooted — he cannot fail to fret and thus upset not only his digestive tract, but the complacency of those about him.

"The one who goes about in 'fear and trembling' is utterly unable to think logically or from cause to effect. Molehills will be magnified to mountains and roadside ditches will deepen into Grand Canyons. One's sense of proportion becomes so distorted that reason and judgment are blotted out of existence. Like an uncultivated field of corn, the weeds destroy the crop."*

Thinking Makes It So

Job, the Hebrew prophet, who personifies the suffering of mortal man, cried: "The thing which I greatly feared is come upon me." This lament is understandable if we believe that thoughts have power over things. Our fear thoughts become as magnetic in attracting trouble as our constructive thoughts in attracting the good.

"By acting *as if* our fears, anxieties, and apprehensions are important, we endow them with importance, we turn

---

* From a newspaper article in the Chicago *Tribune.*

them into realities. They become parasitic growths, existing at the expense of everything that is healthy in us. While we allow them to sap us, we are allowing the nourishment which should go towards expanding growth to be used for feeding monsters, cherishing the freaks and by-blows of the mind instead of its extraordinary and creative elements. So that it is not that one is suddenly given wonderful new powers; by ceasing to let fear hold its frustrating sway *we come into the use of already existing aptitudes which we formerly had no energy to explore.*"*

A recent investigation† reveals the universal existence of fear. One thousand men and women were studied with great care. They were normal people, not the unbalanced types found in psychiatric clinics. They were above average

in both income and education. Fewer than six percent of them were found to be living free from demoralizing worries and fears.

It Is I, I Fear

Of the fifty fears most frequently mentioned, the following five headed the list:

1. My most difficult tendencies are being too self-conscious, being too sensitive, and worrying about what others think of me.

---

* Dorothea Brande, *Wake Up and Live!* pp. 81-82. Simon and Schuster, New York. 1936. Reprinted by permission. Quotation adapted to read "we" instead of "you."

† Harry Walker Hepner, *Psychology Applied to Life and Work*, pp. 7-8. Prentice-Hall, Inc., New York. 1942. Reprinted by permission.

2. My greatest fear and worry is criticism by others.

3. My worst habit is worrying about opinions of others.

4. My greatest need is for more confidence in my own ability.

5. My greatest lack is inability to speak in public.

Bryant S. Hinckley, a contemporary religious leader, illuminates the same problem in these words: "Fear and Faith represent the two great influences which move the human heart . . . . Fear discounts initiative, discourages enterprise, diminishes resourcefulness, weakens the will, and enfeebles the noblest resolves. More failures are due to fear than to any other common cause."*

Fight It

Dr. Frank Crane warns: "Fear reaches out its ghostly hands to strangle you in the nick of the crisis, just when everything depends on you.

"It is fear that tangles your feet, hangs like a millstone around your neck on your journey; it dims your eyes so that you cannot see the truth, roars in your ears until you cannot hear the music all about, fevers your blood, unstrings your nerves, and pours its poison into your cup of life.

"You have one big battle. It is to conquer fear. That done, the world is yours, your own will come to you, and the stars in their course will fight for you."†

---

* "Every Man's Problem," in *Church Section, The Deseret News,* August 9, 1941. Reprinted by permission.
† Quoted in "Every Man's Problems," by Bryant S. Hinckley.

Fear of an audience can turn brave men into timid men, proud and successful men into cowardly men, and cheerful men into sad, depressed, and beaten men. A speaker can no more seed his brain with thoughts of fear and failure and hope for a harvest of success than he can sow thistles and reap golden grain. Fear is the enemy of rational action!

Fear Can Be Conquered

Some veteran speakers declare that fear cannot be completely overcome, and that, even if it could, it would not be desirable. They assert that a bit of fear makes effectiveness possible. With this point of view, the writer heartily disagrees. He believes that this unfortunate attitude tends to keep fear alive. He prefers to follow the admonition of Emerson: "Do the thing you fear to do, and the death of fear is absolutely certain."

The result of applying Emerson's advice is demonstrated in the story of Elmer White, who discovered self-confidence for himself.

He was a man in his forties when he finally mustered the courage to come to a class in public speaking. He was healthy, had a fine family, owned his home, and was successful in his profession. He had a good sense of humor and a capacity for fun. After applying himself with determination for several years, he dashed off the following letter to the author:

"When I began training in public speaking, I had vague hopes that I might be able to develop enough skill to overcome my terrible fears of an audience.

"This ambition now has been realized. I have been elected president of both the service club to which I belong and the state organization of my professional group.

"I enjoy going to the meetings of these organizations now. Before I took work in public speaking, I literally hated to go for fear I would be asked to do something that would require me to speak.

"My fears are now totally gone. I wish all students of speech might be assured that fear can be completely conquered through training and speaking experience."

How did this man overcome his fears and establish self-confidence? He arrived at an understanding of what really happens to the speaker when he faces an audience. He learned that the excitement he felt was not fear and might not be unpleasant;  that to feel an inner stirring was as normal as breathing. It was the price he paid for "being a race horse instead of a cow." There was nothing un-

 natural about it. He admitted that he had the same feeling when he hooked a fish, shot a deer, bought a new car, played handball, or kissed his wife, especially in the moonlight.

Glands and Goose Flesh

Such activities set off a whole train of inner reactions: Two little adrenal glands just above the kidneys discharge their fluid into the blood. This adrenalin quickens and strengthens the action of the heart and the respiratory muscles. The arteries of the abdomen constrict. The sweat glands on the surface of the body begin to secrete perspiration. The tiny muscles about the roots of the hair contract causing "goose flesh." Under the influence of the adrenalin, the liver pours stored-up sugar into the blood. It is evident that the "decks" are being cleared for action. Physiologically, the person is making ready to undertake a challenging activity. It does not mean that he is in the throes of disintegration or that he is in the grip of panic.

Understanding Leads to Control

This understanding solved the mystery for Mr. White concerning the cause of his excitement when he arose to speak. It enabled him to interrupt the fear cycle by positive thinking. You can do the same by applying the suggestions of Dr. Virgil Anderson:

"The speaker should recall his past successes rather than his failures and should look upon himself as being perfectly capable of meeting the present situation adequately. No suggestion that he is inferior, that he is on trial, that it is a life-or-death matter, or that he is in danger of failing should be allowed to enter his head.

"He should be content to do his best and should realize that no more will be expected of him. His hearers he should think of as being people like himself, neither inferior nor superior, but helpful and friendly in their feeling toward him and interested in what he may have to say, not just because he is saying it but because the subject matter appeals to them.

"He should remember that they are not expecting him to exhibit symptoms of stage fright and that in all likelihood they will not be aware of it if he does have a mild attack. The speaker should find comfort in the thought that *stage fright always feels much worse than it looks.*"*

Think of Others

Elmer White turned his thoughts outward, away from himself. He learned that to be self-conscious is to be conscious of the wrong person and that if he were to become adept in social situations he must become conscious of others — of listeners and of audience. He came to regard himself as merely the vehicle for ideas, as a train or plane might be regarded when it is freighted with cargo. As a result he didn't permit his mind to center upon his own feelings. In this way he eliminated apology, excuse-making, and self-abasement.

When fulfilling a speaking engagement where there was a dinner or program ahead of his talk, Mr. White relaxed and enjoyed them. He always determined the exact time he was to appear. He could then turn his thoughts to his speech just a few minutes before his appearance. He casually reviewed his opening, and when he started to talk, he breathed deeply and spoke out slowly and clearly.

If he was a bit uncertain about the sequence of his ideas, he referred to the key-word outline before him. It was typed in large print. When he read a quotation, the double-spaced typing on the card allowed him to keep his attention on the audience rather than on the reading mat-

---

* Virgil A. Anderson, *Training the Speaking Voice*, pp. 215-16. Oxford University Press, New York. 1942. Reprinted by permission.

ter. He held his notes in one hand and moved his thumb down the card. This enabled him to fix his eyes on the right place each time his gaze returned from the audience to pick up the next line. He concentrated all his energies on pleasant and positive factors.

A Self-Confidence Formula

Mr. White acquired self-confidence through a knowledge that he was using right principles. Poise came with the assurance that he was not practising his former errors. This process of building confidence is explained clearly in a practical course in public speaking*: "If you analyze the situation, you will learn that fear is always due to *lack of confidence*. If you fall into the water, you do not fear if you have confidence in your ability to swim to shore. Lack of this confidence would probably cause you to become panic-stricken and drown.

"You analyze the situation, and you learn that lack of confidence exists because of the lack of ability. If you have ability, there is no reason for a lack of confidence. One eliminates the other.

"If lack of ability is responsible for lack of confidence, then it must follow that ability develops confidence. Lack of ability is due to lack of training. Correct *training* will develop the thing that is lacking, *ability*.

"When you analyze the entire formula, you arrive at this decision:

"*Lack of training = lack of ability = lack of confidence = fear.* [LT = LA = LC = F].

---

* F. H. Beckmann, *Practical Public Speaking*, II, 7-8. Beckmann, Hollister and Company, Inc., San Francisco. 1926. Reprinted by permission.

"This leads you to the logical and sensible conclusion that $T = A = C$ [Training = Ability = Confidence], which means that:

"*Correct training develops ability.*
Ability develops confidence.
Confidence eliminates fear."

Preparation Liberates

The problem of how to speak in public is solved only by *preparation*. In addition to training it includes every other effort the speaker can make to insure his own success. More specifically, *preparation* means that the individual must have something to say. According to Professor Mursell, "halting, disjointed, rambling, and pointless utterance comes far more commonly from having nothing to say than from not knowing how to say it."*

The counsel of Henry Ward Beecher to a student at Yale University summarizes a sound approach to the development of self-confidence:

"If you were taking drawing lessons, and attempting to portray the human face, but with so little success as to make it very doubtful what you were trying to do; and if you should look up to your teacher and say to him, 'How shall I increase my ability to draw

---

* James L. Mursell, *Streamline Your Mind*, p. 220. J. P. Lippincott Company. Philadelphia. Reprinted by permission.

faces?' what would he say to you? 'Practice — practice — that will do it.' Preaching is, in one sense, an art. It is a thing to be learned, both in *general principles* and in *practical details*. It is learned by some, as every trade is, much more easily than by others. It is learned by continuous trying and practicing.''*

The will to succeed expresses itself through perseverance. This is impressively stated by Buffon, the French naturalist:

"Most people are willing to do a thing once, many will do it twice, some will do it ten times, a few will do it one hundred times — but I, Buffon, will keep on doing the same thing again and again a thousand times, if necessary, until I have finally done it right!"

---

* *Yale Lectures on Preaching,* p. 49. J. B. Ford and Company, New York. 1872.

CHAPTER III

SPEAK IDEAS WITH LIVE WORDS

SEVERAL YEARS AGO, while the writer was traveling in New Zealand as a missionary, he met a resident on the street of a small town. This individual was full of curiosity about Utah and was soon asking numerous questions: "What is the nature of the country? How was it settled? What do the people believe? How do they live?"

A Little Louder, Please!

In the midst of the conversation, a friend stopped to listen, and then a second, a third, and a fourth. Attracted by the little knot of listeners, others of the townspeople came until an intersection of the street was blocked.

The conversation between the two had begun quite casually and informally. But as the size of the group grew, someone suggested that the missionary talk more loudly and more slowly. Another called out asking the speaker to mount a nearby step so that the group could see, as well as hear. As the crowd increased, the talk became more formal. The questions ceased, and the missionary spoke without interruption about life and customs in his native state.

Just where did the conversation end and the speech begin? In what way did the style of speaking change? Was it when a dozen people gathered? Did mounting the step make any difference? One thing is certain: Any change that crept into the relationship between converser and listeners was one of *degree* rather than of *kind*. At least, the missionary had made a so-called speech without being aware of it. This experience helps explain what is meant by the *conversational mode* — the style of speaking which is best loved by the listener.

Like Talking to the Family

Conversation that becomes a speech is spontaneous and free from display. For the most part, it is quiet but animated and direct — although at times it may become energetic and forceful to express certain ideas and feelings. The speaker is free from self-consciousness and tension, and his manner is simple and forthright. He maintains an intimate *physical, mental, emotional, and spiritual* relationship with his listeners, talking naturally and manifesting a "lively sense of communication." He is at home with his audience as if he were talking with his own family.

Light Up the Fishy Eye

Recently, the writer spoke to a mothers' club. The day was hot and muggy. When the talk was finished, one lady

was heard to exclaim to another: "My, how I wanted to go to sleep, but that speaker watched me so closely I didn't dare." Being direct is the best way in the world to control knitters, doodlers, whisperers, hecklers, and sleepers.

But what is directness? It is keeping the eyes of the speaker focused upon the eyes of the individuals in the audience. It is actually looking at and seeing all of the listeners all the time. Assuming you are the speaker, addressing a small audience, you talk with each member for a few seconds at a time, continually repeating this process. Don't miss a single one! And don't look out the window, stare at the ceiling, or fix your eyes on the floor. Be direct.

In a large audience, directness is gained by picking out certain persons in the various sections of the auditorium and talking personally with them "straight-from-the-shoulder." You talk sense with them and create harmony both intellectually and emotionally. You maintain a movement of thought not only to the audience but also back from it. You watch the expressions on your listeners' faces. You make them feel that they're helping you make your speech and are part of it. It is the "You and I" spirit.

"There is no place on the platform for the impersonal attitude, the fishy eye, the colorless voice. Public speaking demands the personal touch, interest in the listeners, and a very strong sense of talking to them. The audience is made up of human beings, and when this is kept in mind, the speaker is apt to be conversationally direct."*

Effective Speaking Is Like a Gentleman Conversing

Learning to be an effective speaker is basically learning to be as much oneself when talking to a thousand people as when talking to one person. Add to good conversation the power of *preparation*, and the result is force, dignity, and appropriateness required by the occasion.

The key to good delivery is expressed in the word *with*. It is the speaker conveying his idea to the listener — talking, thinking, and feeling *with* the audience, and in

---

* *Basic Field Manual Military Training*, FM 21-5, p. 42. Prepared under direction of Chief of Staff. U.S. Printing Office, Washington, D.C. 1941.

turn, the audience *with* the speaker. He can amplify the *manner* of his speaking without changing its *quality*. He can emulate Wendell Phillips, the famous anti-slavery orator, of whom it was said: "He spoke as a gentleman conversing."

Expression Makes Impression

The practical advice of James Mangan, sales expert, is much to the point when he says: "For every *impression* you make on another, there must be some *expression* on your part. Expression consists in taking everything that is inside you — your spirit, your emotion, your intelligence, and all the rest of your ability — and seeing that it definitely gets *outside you*, to reach as large a number of people as possible. You may be loaded with talent, but it isn't worth two cents until you are able to let others know you have it."*

Think Ideas, Not Words

As in conversation, the speaker should think *ideas*, not words. He should remember that most listeners will accept a clear statement as a true one. He must learn to think with his audience before him, neither reading nor memorizing the words of his talk. This is imperative.

In his popular work, *Streamline Your Mind*, Dr. James L. Mursell says precisely what every student of speech needs to remember — "*Don't try to prepare the exact words of your speech.* Even for the orator of genius this is a handicap. Bourdaloue, one of the great French preachers of the time of Louis XIV, always delivered his sermons with his eyes closed. Asked why this was, he re-

---

* James T. Mangan, *The Knack of Selling Yourself*, p. 33. The Dartnell Corporation, Chicago. 1942. Reprinted by permission.

plied, 'Lest I forget.' The effort of remembering was so great that the memorized words came between him and his audience instead of uniting them. And if this is a weakness in the greatest, it is a fatal defect in the ordinary man. Make a practice of learning your speech off by heart, and you are in the straight pathway towards converting yourself into a human phonograph instead of an effective speaker."*

Don't Let Detail Wag "De Dog"

Mursell also states: "The *detail of English is not very important in speaking.* Several times I have heard men deliver speeches which thrilled their audiences and which everyone, including myself, thought eloquent. Then I have had occasion to edit their remarks for publication from the verbatim record. It was downright illiterate! Spoken and written English are two very different things. Sincerity, directness, and above all, having *something to say* can largely obscure all sorts of verbal crudities."*

Say It Simply

Can you recall enough words to develop and express your ideas? If you know what you want to say, you will find the words. Hundreds of adults tested for vocabulary proficiency were found to be from two to five times more fluent than they thought they were. The build-up-your-vocabulary advocates have oversold their wares. Today the emphasis is shifting to "put it in plain words" and "say it in short sentences." Speech must be instantly understandable. Most of the vocabulary crusaders are preparing their tomes for writers and not for speakers. There is a fundamental

---

* James L. Mursell, *Streamline Your Mind*, pp. 221-22. J. B. Lippincott Company, Philadelphia. 1936. Reprinted by permission.

difference between written and spoken language which is too rarely emphasized.

Nail Big Ideas with Small Words

As a clincher on this point, consider the findings of Colonel Leonard P. Ayres, eminent executive, who collected  thousands of letters written upon every conceivable subject. He tabulated all the words used in these letters and found that they numbered 240,000; but when the different words were counted, they numbered only 2,000. Three hundred words accounted for seventy-five percent of all the writing, and the first 1,000 words on the list accounted for ninety-one percent. The second thousand words, or the more decorative part of the vocabulary, were used only nine percent of the time. In the speeches of Bryan, Ingersoll, Beecher, Conwell, and Grady eighty-nine to ninety-five words of every hundred spoken were one and two syllables. Lincoln's "Gettysburg Address" of 267 words contains only twenty-one words of more than two syllables.

Read the Scriptures for Word Power

Here is an excerpt of 150 words from the Sermon on the Mount. Only one word in fifty contains more than two syllables:

> "Therefore I say unto you, take no thought
> for your life, what ye shall eat, or what ye
> shall drink; nor yet for your body, what ye
> shall put on. Is not the life more than meat,
> and the body than raiment?

"Behold the fowls of the air: for they sow not, neither do they reap, nor gather into barns; yet your heavenly Father feedeth them. Are ye not much better than they?

"Which of you by taking thought can add one cubit unto his stature?

"And why take ye thought for raiment? Consider the lilies of the field, how they grow; they toil not, neither do they spin:

"And yet I say unto you, That even Solomon in all his glory was not arrayed like one of these." (Matt. 6:25-29.)

Use Your Dictionary

Keep your expression spontaneous and earnest, and work to improve your vocabulary. Use the dictionary! Study synonyms. Look up both the meaning and pronunciation of unfamiliar words, and especially verbs. They are the life and power of speech. Be alert to discover new and colorful words. Practice the use of short and specific words. But as a beginning student of speech cease to worry about language. While speaking, think information, ideas, and convictions.

A Few Short Words by Gelett Burgess

A master of expression is Gelett Burgess. The following paragraphs reflect the power of short words and simple sentences:

"Our speech has lost force by too much use of long words. A lot of old short words now sound queer and crude. We do not use them when we try to speak well. But short words are strong words. They would help us to make our talk more clean-cut, fresh, and hale; they give it salt and tang.

"When we are tried sore, when we faint with fear, or pain stings, or we blaze with wrath, then we cry out: 'Help me! Come quick!' We snarl, 'You lie, you cur!' We yell, 'The house is on fire!' We wail, 'Oh, woe is me!' or moan, 'She is gone. She has left me. She does not love me!'

"And when we are blithe and gay, too, we do not use long words that reek of books. We say: 'Oh, joy! I love you. Come and kiss me. Be mine!'

"Bad words are all short, too. They bite. They are vile, but they do not slide or hide. They say what they mean.

"For short words come from deep down in our hearts, not from our brains. They are like the bones of speech that make talk firm and hard. Like blood that gives life. Long words are the fat and thews and skin that make speech fair of form. But with a lack of short words what one says has less truth and zest. Less youth, too.

"Why not bring some of those old words back to life? They would be as stout as rough oaths to make our talk force home what we mean. They would be as sharp as slang, too, that has pash and pep to dart, flash, pinch with the quick play of wit.

"Friend, read the Good Book and see how clear, how stark, how crisp are the short words of our great tongue. They are the words of might."*

---

* Reproduced from a newspaper article entitled, "Five Hundred Short Words."

Make It Short and Sweet

If you wish to be heard with enjoyment and ease, state your ideas simply by following these suggestions:

1. *Select the right word,* one that is accurate and concrete. The power of such a word is aptly described by the poet:

   Oh, a word is a gem, or a stone, or a song,
   Or a flame, or a two-edged sword,
   Or a rose in bloom, or a sweet perfume,
   Or a drop of gall, is a word.*

2. *Keep the sentences short.* The extensive studies of Rudolf Flesch show conclusively that literary and scientific English are difficult for the average listener. The following is a tabulation of his findings:†

AVERAGE SENTENCE LENGTH IN WORDS

Very Easy	8 or less
Easy	11
Fairly Easy	14
Standard	17
Fairly Difficult (literary English)	21
Difficult	25
Very Difficult (scientific English)	29 or more

   The average sentence in *You Can Learn to Speak!* is eighteen words long.

3. *Speak with animation.* Said Joseph Conrad: "Give me the right word and the right accent, and I will move the world."

---

* James T. Baker, *The Short Speech,* p. 33. Prentice-Hall, Inc., New York. 1932. Reprinted by permission.
† *The Art of Plain Talk,* p. 38. Harper and Brothers Publishers, New York. 1946. Reprinted by permission.

CHAPTER IV

LESS MOTION FOR MORE EMOTION

OBSERVE THE WISDOM of the most down-to-earth advice ever given on the subject of speech delivery: *Fill up the barrel. Knock out the bung. Let nature caper.* Follow the admonition of the colored preacher:

> Read yourself full;
> Think yourself straight;
> Pray yourself hot;
> Let yourself go !

Put the Tears in to Get Them Out

An editorial in the New York *Sun* points out that "you don't find feelings in words unless there are feelings in the man who uses them. With all their apparent independence they seem to be little vessels that hold in some puzzling fashion *exactly what is put into them.* You can put tears into them, as though they were so many little buckets; and you can hang smiles along them, like Monday's clothes on the line, or you can starch them with facts and stand them up like a picket fence; but *you can't get the tears out unless you first put them in.* Art won't put them there . . . if they aren't in the man, no technical skill will supply them."*

A Good Teacher Is Usually a Good Speaker

In the rating of teachers by their students, no deficiency in the personality of the teacher is so often mentioned as a lack of animation, vitality, vivacity, enthusiasm, and dynamics. The importance of color and life in communication cannot be overemphasized or overrated. The harm done by dull, routine, lifeless speaking, teaching, and preaching is *appalling*.

Quicken the Spirit

The answer to what your speech does to your audience will more than likely be found in what the delivery of the speech does to you. Henry Ward Beecher, one of America's greatest pulpit orators, told the divinity school students in his Yale Lectures: "You do not want an argument for the sake of an argument. You do not want a sermon that is as perfect a machine as a machine can be, unless it *does* something. *You want the people,* and the shortest and surest way to get them is the best way." And that shortest and best way is to have your idea, conviction, proposition, get you first. It must be a vital, throbbing, living thing for you.

Kindle the Will

Stuart Sherman, a former teacher at the University of Illinois, explained what the attitude of speakers and

* New York *Sun,* March 16, 1890.

teachers should be: There is no *routine teaching*, and there should be no *routine teachers*. The real teacher "must never conceive that divulging information is the end of his work. His important task is to kindle the will, the emotions, the imagination; and to sensitize the mind, fill it with light, make it desirous and eager." Real teachers never "go into the classroom and lay out their intellectual commodities with the air of a languid clerk in a dry-goods store, saying, 'Take it or leave it, as you like.'"*

Alive to the Tip of His Tongue

Hamlin Garland describes the speaking power of Robert G. Ingersoll, one of the world's most persuasive men, with these unforgettable words: "There was something hypnotic in his rhythm . . . . His effect on his hearers was magical . . . .

"A large part of his power lay in the fact that he vitalized every word, every syllable. He thought each sentence out at the moment he gave it utterance. He was alive to the tip of his tongue. He did not permit his organs of speech to proceed mechanically. He remained in control . . . . He taught me the value of speaking."† This statement emphasizes a basic rule in speaking. No matter how perfect his articulation or how flawless his grammar, *the speaker must think as he speaks and understand the significance of every idea.* Only then will his listeners understand and believe.

---

* Stuart Sherman, *Shaping Men and Women*, pp. 28-29. Doubleday, Doran and Company, Inc., New York. 1928. Reprinted by permission.

† Hamlin Garland, *Roadside Meetings*, pp. 45-46. The Macmillan Company, New York. 1930. Reprinted by permission.

Mannerisms Are Your Toughest Competitor

The speaker must work to eliminate the mannerisms and peculiarities that divert the attention of an audience away from his message. Among the worst are the irritating "er's," "ah's," "mm's," "and-a's," "but's," and "so's," generally known as word-whiskers. Speakers addicted to the habit of mouthing sounds without regard to sense or meaning can annoy listeners until their nerves begin to fall to pieces.

X Marks the Spot

At a renowned middle-western university, a professor who was an expert on American history expected his students to take copious notes. I sat next to a bright boy who was always busy enough, but whose notebook was full of crosses that looked like ballot marks on election day. You see, the professor lectured like this: "How . . . ah . . . indeed . . . er-a . . . could it be . . . ah . . . otherwise, . . . er-a when . . . ah . . . all the taxes . . . er-a . . . since . . . ah . . . 1781 did not . . . er-a . . . amount . . . er-a to $750,000 . . . ah."

My neighbor industriously made an x-mark rhythmically with every "ah" or "er-a" launched by the professor. One day in a joking way I said, "That's a wonderful system of note taking you have — so efficient." He looked at me with scorn and retorted, "Notes be darned; I just put down how many times the old goat goes 'ah.' It's so bad, I can't resist counting the number of such babblings. I don't know what's the matter with him. I thought he was supposed to know what he was talking about. Why, he went 'uh' seventy times in ten minutes. He nearly drives me crazy."

Pause Silently

The word-whisker habit can be broken. Hundreds of students have succeeded, first, by becoming critical of their own verbal beards and then by shaving them off with something specific to say, by learning to keep their minds on their subjects, and by being determined to pause silently instead of audibly.

Fill Your Mind but Empty Your Pockets

There are countless other distracting habits that concentration can correct — if your best friends and teachers tell you what they are. They range all the way from playing aimlessly with your notes and clothing to scratching your chin, rubbing your face, pulling at your ears, and massaging your hair; from rattling money and keys in your pocket to twirling your watch chain and slipping your ring on and off your finger. If you are a victim of such habits, fill your mind with ideas to express, then empty your pockets and remove your ring and watch chain until you have finished speaking. And don't saw the air with the same old gesture. Your listeners may wish that you would saw trees instead of their nerves.

On Again Off Again

One day a speaker came to the university from the commonwealth of South Africa. He had spoken only a short time when the impulse to read a passage hit him. Ceremoniously he took his glasses from the case and mounted them on his nose. But at that crucial moment another idea struck him, and he decided not to read, so he removed his glasses and twirled them vigorously between his fingers. To read or not to read . . .

that seemed to be the question. Jittery indecision caused him to repeat the process of mounting and dismounting his pince-nez for a full fifteen minutes. No fewer than forty or fifty times did this master-of-his-art repeat this thrilling performance until every member of his audience developed a swivel neck trying to follow the speaker's gyrations.

As Others See You

See yourself as others see you, and you will fast eliminate distracting mannerisms. They can ruin a good speech. Don't blow your nose, clear your throat, press your clothing, drink from the glass on the speaker's stand, clean your glasses — at least not more than once or twice. And don't slouch over the speaker's stand or continually shift your weight, teeter, fidget, or shuffle your feet, jerk your head, shrug your shoulders, or pace back and forth like a lion in a cage. The reason for this obvious advice is graphically depicted in the following statement: "A speaker is seen as well as heard. And we naturally expect that what we see in his behavior as he speaks will agree with what he is saying. *Communication is not carried on solely by means of words.* There can be no real animation in speech if the bodily means of expression do not *cooperate* with the vocal means. Physical expression is often more accurate and more immediate in conveying meaning than words. Words may be ambiguous, but a wink, a lifted eyebrow, a dropped jaw, a blush, a smile, a scowl are not easily mistaken.''*

Have Mercy On the Audience

The speaker should remember that his listeners will perform subconsciously and intra-organically all his movements and actions. They will become weary if he strides up and down the platform. They will become verbally prostrate if he stutters and stumbles over his words. They will become tired out if he stands perfectly still in his tracks like a fox or rabbit "freezing" to escape notice.

The speaker must eliminate his disagreeable mannerisms if he wishes to put his audience at ease. His freedom of action provides their muscular release. It is true: *What the speaker does, the people in the audience will also tend to do!*

Enjoyment Begins with the Speaker

The speaker who achieves effectiveness must find real enjoyment in his own speaking. He must not accept grudgingly or fearfully the invitation to speak. Rather, he should respond as if he were invited to fish in the deep, clear, waters of the Yellowstone or to hunt for the wary moose in the Canadian uplands. The person who enjoys the opportunities of speech making is less likely to be a bore. Without the challenge and verve of enjoyment, showmanship and mastery are impossible.

---

* Wayland M. Parrish, *The Teacher's Speech*, p. 25. Harper & Brothers Publishers, New York. 1939. Reprinted by permission.

Those who dance well like to dance. Those who sing well love to sing. Those who golf well love to play golf. Those who develop proficiency in anything—flower-raising, stamp collecting, flying, sculpturing, woodworking, reading, or *speaking* thrill to the opportunity to practice their skills.

Enter Into the Joy of Your Skill

The gist of the whole matter can be summed up in the parable of the talents. All went well with those servants who increased their resources. They were bidden to enter into the joy of their lord. But for the servant who took no joy in his opportunity and "was afraid and went and hid his talent in the earth," it was a sad story of reproach and remorse. Today's crowded world offers no finer achievement to any of us than to acquire enjoyment in the skill of speaking, whether we speak to small or large groups. From the doing comes the skill, and from the skill comes joy.

So . . .

Once more, speak clearly, if you speak at all;
Carve every word before you let it fall;

Don't start your speech with that old worn-out "well,"
But, from the first, your ringing message tell.

Cut out the "uh's" and "ah's," two thirds of
　　the "very's" too;
Omit most "then's" and "so's," and better you will do.

The climax reached at last, in simple words and neat,
Be sure you stop at once and calmly take your seat.*

---

* James T. Baker, *The Short Speech*, p. 51. Prentice-Hall, Inc., New York. 1932. Reprinted by permission.

CHAPTER V

EVEN I AM LEARNING TO SPEAK

EDITOR'S NOTE: In this chapter and the one following, the author tells his own story: how he became interested in learning to express himself and how he systematized the gathering of examples, quotations, and ideas, many of which form a substantial part of this volume.

Slow of Speech

When I arrived from the country to attend a city high school, I was a self-conscious boy — afraid of school, teachers, classes, and girls. At every new situation my heart beat fast, and I perspired.

My recitations before the class would blurt out in jumbled fashion, and my breath would come shorter and shorter until I couldn't produce a sound. It was a strange and harrowing experience.

These events are related for two reasons: First, to compare my lack of confidence at school with the strange ordeal an inexperienced speaker suffers when facing an audience. [Entirely new circumstances are usually faced with some feeling of panic, but the individual who believes he has achieved some success gains confidence.] Second, to inspire some hope in your ultimate achievement, if you are fearful of your native ability.

Because of encouragement from parents and friends, I took a course in public speaking during the third year of high school. The class studied Woolbert's *Fundamentals of Speech*, but what we read about speaking principles was not nearly so important as what we did. We spoke under the kindest and most encouraging of circumstances.

That first teacher was a jewel. He never permitted us to feel failure, unless our own neglect or carelessness made negative criticism the only honest way.

Stumbling Steps

That first speaking experience was a nightmare. After preparing for several days and late into the night, and repeating the talk during most of the mile walk to school, I jumped when my name was called. Rushing to the front of the class, I began to talk before I took my position. I didn't pause to meet the eyes of the students nor did I wait until I had taken a deep breath. I plunged into my talk as a passenger on a sinking ship might leap into a seething torrent. So I forgot most of my ideas. I talked in a nervous, high-pitched voice. I gestured wildly. I was back to my seat in a few feverish seconds, not knowing for sure what I had said. The students were laughing hilariously. I was mortified and crushed. I decided to quit. I couldn't take it.

Then this teacher did an excellent thing. He called me into his office for a conference. He said the talk was really better than I thought it had been. He mentioned that I had apparently worked hard in preparation. The topic of my speech had been the humor of Lincoln. In a book on this subject which a friend had given me for Christmas, was the statement that he who can make two blades of grass grow where there is one is a great man, but that he who can bring forth a laugh where there is none is a greater man. I had tried to repeat those words and to remember some other words from the book that explained why. I had no examples of Lincoln's humor; only some general statements about its importance and his skill in using it.

Earning the Right to Speak

The instructor reviewed my talk with me. Then he made a point I have never forgotten. He said no one could become a speaker by depending upon another's resources. Every person must develop his own. On any subject that a speaker talks upon, he must earn the right to speak.

The instructor asked me what I had done in my short lifetime. "Nothing!" I complained. He reassured me that merely to live was something. Of what had my living consisted?

Well, I told him that as a boy I had delivered groceries in a red wagon. I pulled weeds and milked cows. I bought a pair of rabbits for ten dollars from an eastern firm. I borrowed the money from my father. As soon as the rabbits began reproducing as only rabbits can, the company went broke, and I had to pay for the return of the rabbits I had already shipped; this called for frugal saving. I raised a prize pig at thirteen, and at fourteen I won a blue ribbon at the Utah State Fair for an entry of yellow corn.

One July day, while hauling grain from our dry farm, my uncle unknowingly threw a rattlesnake on a bundle of wheat up to me on the wagon. I knocked the snake to the ground and then helped to kill it. I kept the eight rattles and one button for years. I had a hair-raising scare with a runaway horse. I was almost killed when thrown from a careening wagon into a pond between two heavy spray barrels. I learned how to teach a calf to drink from a bucket, how to hive a swarm of migrating bees, how to catch gophers in the field and rats in the barn. I picked and crated fruit of all kinds and helped my father sell and deliver it to our customers in the city.

The instructor soon had me feeling that my background was interesting, and that these experiences could be the substance of future talks before the class. No more was I to talk from vaguely remembered materials that I did not understand. The instructor emphasized that I should read whatever I could find on subjects of my experiences. When I found interesting information, I should keep it for future use.

Experience

This wise teacher unlocked the door to my interest in public speaking. It may be that my ambition was aroused at an early age. But the process of learning to speak is the same at any age. Success is governed by calling upon one's firsthand experiences, developing basic interests, and supplementing these by what can be gleaned from reading and listening.

After high school, I served as a missionary to New Zealand. Here I learned to quote from both Scriptures and religious leaders. Also I kept a diary of my own thoughts and experiences. These were useful in my homecoming report.

My formal speech training was resumed at the university. Here again I used personal experiences as source material. For illustration, I brought grass skirts, greenstone, and native robes to class and told how they were made and used. I demonstrated the official Maori greeting of nose rubbing and related the experience of meeting native chiefs and political celebrities. I talked of the customs, traditions, and culture of the Maoris. On a modest scale, these talks were like those of explorers and travelers. They were supplemented by firsthand experiences and materials gleaned from the anthropology and history of the country. In fact, these speeches defrayed some educational expenses during the depression of the thirties. Never have I made an effective talk that did not stem from some deep-rooted interest, whether on religion, human relations, salesmanship, or cancer.

Loosening the Tongues of Others

The lessons learned from my first instructor have helped a number of college and business people. For example, a man came to me almost panic-stricken. He was a prominent leader in his town. The alumni of the high school from which he had graduated some years back had honored him by electing him president of their association. A new gymnasium for the school was to be dedicated. He, among others, must make a short talk. To refuse meant humiliation and loss of prestige. His first impulse was to write a pretentious address and commit it to memory, but he was not an educator or a so-called intellectual.

He wanted to feel comfortable in what he did, so he came to seek advice. He had no idea of what he could say. We spent half an hour recalling his past experiences. The result was a talk that was neither written nor memorized. He didn't make a great speech. (Most occasions don't require great speeches. These are better made by the Websters and Lincolns.) The following is about what he said to the townspeople on the night of the dedication of the gymnasium:

A Dream Come True

"The alumni have backed the building of our new gymnasium from the very first. We helped to arouse enthusiasm for it. We helped to raise the funds. We have been interested in the plans and the construction every step of the way. Tonight, we are proud and happy — along with all of you, who have also helped — that our dream has come true.

"I can remember when I played basketball for this high school. Some of you old teammates in the audience played with me in the opera house. On cold nights like this one tonight, we had no heat in our dressing room. The small furnace in the building supplied only enough for the spectators upstairs. So it was all piped up to them. As we dressed and undressed before and after the games, we shivered and shook. But we were perfect gentlemen — that is, after the games were over. We always permitted the visiting team to shower first in the hot water that came from a monkey stove of limited capacity. When our turn came, only cold water remained. Most of us survived the games, but the memory of those showers still gives me a chilly feeling.

"This new and beautiful gymnasium changes all of this. And are we oldsters thrilled! We know our boys and girls now have the advantages required to achieve new heights of athletic glory."

This man didn't make excuses or apologize for his lack of speaking ability. He said what he had to say and sat down. An audience enjoys the memories of yesterday. What he said about the old opera house was appropriate, and it prepared the audience for his brief inspirational conclusion. It was a good speech and did him credit. He might have said more profound things, but they would have seemed strained and unnatural. He was wise to leave that responsibility to the orator of the evening.

From Fright to Freedom

On another occasion a man of wealth and position in our city came to me half sick. His worry was stirring up his ulcers. He had to speak before a national convention on the operation of small mines. Since mining was his business, he knew the subject from every viewpoint. But he had written out a highly technical paper full of complex sentences and abstractions. It would have been laborious to read and boring to hear.

Here is the formula he followed. He sent his paper to the editor of the mining magazine where it was to be published. He had the chairman of the meeting explain this to the audience and remind them that the paper would be available in the published proceedings. He then spoke on two or three fundamental principles in the operation of a small mine. In a pleasant manner he related vivid experiences of his own and of his associates. This procedure put his mind entirely at ease. He even had a little fun and injected some humor which his audience enjoyed.

Hardly one person in ten listens to a learned address with concentration or profit. Hence, the speaker should not try to cover all the points related to a subject, or set the world right, or answer all objections, or plug up all the loopholes, or solve all the problems, or try to make a reputation for himself. Rather, he should sound like a human being whose first interest is consideration for his listeners.

If you still feel uneasy about discarding your manuscript, consider the advice of a distinguished scholar and speaker, who wrote the introduction to the second volume of *Modern Eloquence*:

"You fear that you may lose your thread, or your logical connection, or some valuable fact or illustration. But you may be sure that neither thread nor logic, nor argument is so important to the audience as that they should be kept in entire sympathy with yourself, that the magnetic contact, or whatever we call it, should be unbroken. The chances are that nobody will miss what you leave out, if you forget anything; but you will lose much if you forego the continuous and confiding attention given to a speaker who is absolutely free."*

As has been well said: "A speech should be like the leaping of a fountain, not the pumping of a pump."

---

* Thomas Wentworth Higginson, "Hints on Speech Making," in *Modern Eloquence*, II, xix. Lincoln Scholarship Fund Edition, New York. 1928.

CHAPTER VI

RESOURCES UNLIMITED

FEW ARE ASKED to speak merely because of their resonant voice, statuesque appearance, or magnetic personality. That these factors are important, in whatever degree they may be possessed, no one will deny.

An Englishman exclaimed, when he first saw Daniel Webster: "No man can be as great as Daniel Webster looks." To be able to make an impression like that was surely no handicap, but it was only a small part of Webster's success. When he was asked how much time he had spent in his famous reply to Hayne, Webster exclaimed, "All my life!" The great oratorical classic was not the result of a sudden inspiration, but the product of a lifetime of study, meditation, and analysis.

Too Late Means Too Little

Webster had been preparing himself for years in advance of the actual speaking occasion and on specific subjects. The same was true of Beecher and countless others. To wait until one is asked to talk before beginning to prepare is too late. Usually such invitations are extended on short notice. Then the speaker is in a dither, under strain, and the talk is only mildly successful, if at all, and the speaker resolves that he'll never do it again, even if he is asked — which isn't likely.

Webster discovered that his interest was the law and politics. He fought against disheartening fear of an audience. He had ideas, knowledge, illustrations, and facts. These, along with taking advantage of every opportunity to talk, enabled him to overcome his fears and project himself completely into every speaking situation.

You may not aspire to become a Webster. But the process of learning to speak is basically the same for all people. Like Webster, you will be asked to speak, not because of your looks, but because of your specific preparation on certain subjects.

Develop new areas of interest now and systematize the knowledge you already have. The writer has hundreds of cards filed away on many subjects. These enable him to talk on short notice. And this preparation is the reason he is asked to speak. He is seldom requested to talk on subjects outside the fields of his interest. Here is his account of the birth of a speech, just as it happened.

A Speech Is Born

A beloved member of my family died of cancer. It was a tragic experience. In a desperate effort to save her life, I searched the nation for possible treatments and cures and discovered some startling facts. Early cancer in a majority of cases is curable. But forty-nine percent of all Americans, according to a survey conducted by the University of Michigan, do not know a single one of the seven danger signals of cancer. The cause of the disease is unknown, and money needs to be raised for research, as well as for the education of the public.

Join the crusade against cancer!

I became interested. I clipped and saved every article on the subject. I visited the Sloan-Kettering Institute in New York. I reviewed my own experience. I studied ways of combining the principles of salesmanship to instruct workers on how to sell the program of the American Cancer Society to the public.

One day I was asked to talk to the workers of the local cancer society. National officers were present. That was the beginning. One person told another. I have since made talks over the whole nation and have broadcast nearly a hundred more speeches by transcription.

Here Is Your Chance

If you teach a class for your church, if you have hobbies, if you run a business, or anything else, begin now to file away systematically materials about your interests. You may be astonished at the ultimate outcome. Your subjects may be as varied as life itself. Famous talks on the lyceum have been delivered on pigs, the mustache, keys to success, the Hawaiian Islands, the typical Dutchman, big blunders, penguins, Alaska, fish, Indians, our wives, Yankee notions, the ideal woman, the legal profession, the Fourth of July, and the North Pole. It is not the subject but the speaker and his fascinating facts, unusual anecdotes, and striking illustrations that count. These he collects and files.

Where to discover your interests and how to amass relevant information are told in the story of an obscure spinster woman who insisted that she "never had a chance."* One night she muttered these words to Dr. Louis Agassiz,

---

*Told in a speech class by Nancy Salisbury, whose father, a banker, obtained the story from a publication of the American Institute of Banking.

distinguished naturalist, after one of his lectures in London. In response to her complaint he replied, "You say, Madam, you never had a chance? What do you do?"

"I am single and help my sister run a boardinghouse."

"What do you do?" he asked again.

"I skin potatoes and chop onions."

He said, "Madam, where do you sit during these interesting but homely duties?"

"On the bottom steps of the kitchen stairs."

"Where do your feet rest?"

"On the glazed bricks."

"What is a glazed brick?"

"I don't know, sir."

He said, "How long have you been sitting there?"

"Fifteen years."

"Madam, here is my personal card. Would you kindly write me concerning the nature of a glazed brick?"

Curiosity *a la Femme*

She went home and explored the dictionary to discover that a brick was a piece of baked clay. That definition seemed too simple to send to Dr. Agassiz, so after the dishes were washed, she went to the library and in an encyclopedia read that a glazed brick is vitrified kaolin and hydrous-aluminum silicate. She didn't know what that meant, but she was curious and found out. She took the word *vitrified* and read all she could find on it. She visited museums. She moved out of the basement of her life into a wonderful new world on the wings of *vitrified*, and having started, she took the word *hydrous*, studied geology, went back to the time when God started the world, and laid the clay beds.

One Sunday afternoon she went to a brickyard where she found an intelligent watchman who told her the history of more than 120 kinds of bricks and tiles and why there have to be so many. Then she sat down and wrote thirty-six pages on the subject of glazed bricks and tiles. Back came a letter from Louis Agassiz:

"Dear Madam: This is the best article I have ever seen on the subject. If you will kindly change the three words marked with an asterisk, I will have it published and pay you for it."

A short time later there came a letter that brought $250.00, and on the bottom of this letter was this query in lead pencil: "What was under those bricks?" She had learned the value of time and answered with a single word, "Ants."

He wrote back and said, "Tell me about the ants,"  and she began to study ants. She found there are between 1,800 and 2,500 different kinds. There are ants so tiny that you could put three, head to head, on the head of a pin and have standing room left over, for ants; ants an inch long that march in solid armies a half mile wide, driving everything ahead of them; ants that are blind; ants that get wings on the afternoon of the day they die; ants that build ant hills so tiny that you can cover one with a lady's silver thimble; peasant ants that keep cows to milk and deliver the fresh milk to the apartment houses/of the aristocratic ants of the neighborhood.

After wide reading, much microscopic work, and deep study, she sat down and wrote Dr. Agassiz 360 pages on the subject. He published the book and sent her the money, and she went to visit all the lands of her dreams on the proceeds of her work.

As you read this story, do you feel acutely that all of us are sitting with our feet on vitrified kaolin and hydrous-aluminum silicate, with ants under it? Lord Chesterton answers for you: *"There are no uninteresting things; there are only uninterested people!"*

Write It Down

William Allen White, famous as the editor of the *Emporia Gazette*, never went to a business conference or a dinner party or even an ordinary meal without a note pad in his pocket or beside his plate. New bits of information, witty remarks, wise sayings, anecdotes, and personal observations were all recorded. He later discarded many of the comments and ideas, but one thought or apt illustration was worth all the effort.

Ideas are sensitive. They leave us if they are not made welcome. Every one of us should maintain a hospitality service, all for the purpose of making flitting thought and illustration feel at home.

In building a reference file, begin with your own personal experiences. These are the richest materials of speech making. They establish a feeling of authority and confidence in the speaker.

Treasure Hunt

Most of us are like Lord Shaftesbury, who wrote in his diary in 1854: " 'Very busy. Little time for thought, none for reading. Oftentimes look at a book and long for it as a donkey for a carrot.' That may be our defense. We are so much occupied that all our constructive thinking is consumed in obtaining the wherewithal for our material comforts."*

The truth may be that we consume our time with the wrong things — the funnies, movies, newspapers, radio, and television. Temperate indulgence in these pastimes may be recreational, but most of us occupy so much of our leisure in this way that we starve our twelve billion brain cells on a diet of froth. We forget that "one of the differences between beefsteak and Beethoven is that, when you've eaten the beefsteak, your plate is bare; when you've partaken of Beethoven, there's more Beethoven than you had before. It's the modern miracle of the loaves and fishes. These loaves and fishes come back to you in so many forms."†

If we all loved reading the literature of our great tongue as did Channing Pollock, we too would know Mark Twain, Kipling, Dickens, Hawthorne, Emerson, and all

---

* Mildred Peabody, "Court New Impressions," in *Think*, August 1949, p. 13. Reprinted by permission.

† Channing Pollock, *The Adventures of a Happy Man*, p. 116. Thomas Y. Crowell Company, New York. 1945. Reprinted by permission.

the others. Like him we would thrill to the discovery of literary gems. After reading Sir Conan Doyle, Pollock decided that at the first opportunity he would be as gallant as the archers, one of whom was asked to volunteer for a service of great danger by advancing from the ranks.

When the captain looked up, the line was unbroken. "I'm sorry," he announced. "What is to be done means almost certain death, but I thought *one* man might step forward."

The sergeant saluted and replied, "The whole company stepped forward, sir!"

Finders Keepers

Pollock emphasized: "At eighteen, I believed in a world like that, and sometimes, I still believe in it. Passionately, with all my heart and soul, I wanted to be worthy of such a world, and I still do. At twenty, I was reading Ruskin on railway trains, and Emerson while waiting for theater managers in one-night stands. I quite understood that crowd which went to the Battery to meet the clipper-ship bringing the last installment of *The Old Curiosity Shop*, and that, unable to restrain itself until the boat docked, cried across the water to her first officer, 'Is Little Nell dead?'

"Through the busy years of my youth and middle-age, I have read every day, and every spare moment, in subways, in offices, in the bath and in bed — read with a consuming curiosity, with an avid desire to learn, with a delight in reading such as is to be had, perhaps, from nothing else on earth.

"For me, and for most other readers, courage and nobility and romance are undying. All else may change, diminish, grow ugly and mean, but, as John A. Holmes wrote in a recent issue of the London *Saturday Review*:*

> 'Every day in books
> Rip Van Winkle lies asleep,
> Moby Dick patrols the deep
> Every day in books.

> 'Tall windmills turn in Spain
> Where, across an empty plain,
> Rides the rusty knight in vain
> Every day in books.

> 'Falstaff laughs, and Hamlet dreams;
> Camelot is all it seems;
> Kubla Khan in Xanadu
> Hears the river running through,
> And Marco Polo sails away;
> Mr. Pickwick has his say;
> Troy is falling every day
> Every day in books.

> 'You can pass, and I can pass,
> Toward them, through the Looking Glass
> Every day, in books.' "

Quote, Unquote

Quotations have been used throughout this book to indicate how the great thoughts of others can complement one's own expression and to guide the reader to rich sources of illustration.

---

* Pollock, *op. cit.*, pp. 117-18.

To employ the well-expressed thoughts of others and give proper credit is not to lack originality. Churchill used the phrase "blood, toil, tears, and sweat," in his speech accepting the post of Prime Minister. John Donne, English poet of the seventeenth century, in his "First Anniversary" poem said,

> "That 'tis in vaine to dew, or mollifie
> It with thy teares, or sweat, or blood."

Robert Browning's "Ixion" has this: "Tears, sweat, blood — each spasm, ghastly once, glorified now."

Churchill undoubtedly had read these lines. His originality consisted in giving new value to something already known, in bringing together existing ideas and linking them in new ways, and in looking at familiar lines and seeing them in connection with a new need. Originality always grows out of what we know.

The individual who is to become a speaker must not only read in the fields of his interests but must also record and file the most pertinent facts and examples.

Keep this in mind — any information or material you acquire from whatever source must become your own in thought and understanding if it is to help you as a speaker. Dale Carnegie once said: "All art is autobiographical. You can only write what you are; you can only sing what you are; you can only speak what you are. If you are an architect, you can only plan the kind of building you get out of your own personality."*

Manual for Instructors, p. 9. Dale Carnegie Institute, New York. 1945. Reprinted by permission. See *Public Speaking and Influencing Men in Business*, by Dale Carnegie. Association Press, New York. 1943.

Reap in Many Fields

Finally, the individual who wants to prepare for speaking must also learn from conversation. It not only clarifies his own thinking but also enables him to reap from specialists in many fields. Conversation is good because in the words of Oliver Wendell Holmes, "It brings our thought out into the open, as a boy turns his pockets inside out to see what is in them."

A Card Game Worth Winning

The material for this book was first assembled on 5" x 8" cards. It was collected over a period of many years, and was filed under such headings as *Conversation*, *Animation*, *Illustrations*, *Vocabulary*, and so on. When the time came to compose a chapter, the writer selected from a superabundance of fact and illustration the most appropriate citations to fit the outline, just as one might do when preparing a talk.

ILLUSTRATIONS (uses of)

Lincoln, in a letter to Colonel John D. Van Buren, said:

"I believe I have the popular reputation of being a storyteller, but I do not deserve the name in its general sense; for it is not the story itself but its purpose, or effect, that interests me. I often avoid a long and useless discussion by others or a laborious explanation on my own part by a short story that illustrates my point of view. So, too, the sharpness of a refusal or the edge of a rebuke may be blunted by an appropriate story, so as to save the wounded feeling and yet serve the purpose. No, I am not simply a storyteller, but storytelling as an emollient saves me much friction and distress."

(Letter written June 26, 1863, found in *The Lincoln Encyclopedia*, p. 247, compiled by Archer H. Shaw. The Macmillan Company, New York. 1950.)

When you know your subject, audience, and purpose, examine your file and arrange before you appropriate clippings from magazines and newspapers and quotations from books. The material selected, if not already transferred to cards, should be typed on them for convenient use.

Cards of 5" x 8" in size are recommended because the typing can be double spaced for easy reading and contain an unabridged quotation. If it is necessary to use both sides, mark "over" on the bottom of the card and insert it into the typewriter so that what was the top on the front side becomes the bottom on the other. When using the card in a talk, merely flip it over instead of turning it around. This simplifies handling.

Put Your Collecting Instincts to Work

When I first began to file materials, I used an alphabetical index. Notes on *Faith, Fear, Freedom*, etc., all were put under F, and on *Peace, Personality, Public Relations*, etc., all under P and so on throughout the alphabet. As the file grew, I bought blank index cards and printed subject heads on them. Separate entries were made for each of the expanded subjects and a careful system of cross referencing begun.

As materials are amassed and the number of items under a single head becomes unwieldy, the subject is again subdivided. Once begun, the cataloguing of materials becomes a most captivating hobby, and one that enriches personal resources. Those items which you retain on cards become nuggets of thought and are like money in the bank — always ready when you need them.

When copying a quotation on a card, list the full name of the author, title of the book, publisher, date of publication, and page number. If in doubt about whether you should record the reference, do it anyway, for that is the one you are certain to want. You can waste hours trying to find something you have passed over. If you haven't time to copy, clip from the newspapers and magazines that are not being saved in some orderly manner. Record the name of the paper or magazine, the date of publication, and the writer if he has a byline.

Surely, it takes time. But that's why so many people fail. They don't take the time or make the effort to succeed. They'd rather make excuses, which are futile, silly, or hurtful.

Take the time.

Make the effort.

Reap the reward !

CHAPTER VII

ILLUSTRATIONS OPEN THE WINDOWS OF THE MIND

"THEY SAY I tell a great many stories; I reckon I do, but I have found in the course of a long experience that common people . . . are more easily informed through the medium of a broad illustration than in any other way, and as to what the hypercritical few may think, I don't care."* These are the words of Abraham Lincoln.

The Lawyers Found It Out

Experience shows that in addition to the common people, the hypercritical few also are more effectively informed by illustration.

"Many years ago Professor C. C. Langdell demonstrated that principles of law should not be taught in the abstract but by the case method. Since then every law school has adopted it. The students are given actual cases in legal history, and from them the guiding rules are derived. The accumulation of illustrations, each containing in its variety of facts the same principle, inscribes the point indelibly upon the mind."†

Students of the law are generally disciplined in reasoning and resourcefulness. If it is better to teach them through illustration, how imperative it is to address all listeners in the same way! Skilled speakers recognize that people think in pictures and remember illustrations.

---

* Spoken to Chauncey M. Depew, quoted in *Lincoln's Own Yarns and Stories*, p. xvii. The John C. Winston Co. Chicago.

† Louis Nizer, *Thinking on Your Feet*, p. 25. Liveright Publishing Corporation, New York. 1940. Reprinted by permission.

It Is Like . . .

Henry Ward Beecher supports the point of view of Lincoln and Langdell. Said he: "I have seen an audience time and again, follow an argument doubtfully, laboriously, almost suspiciously, and look at one another, as much as to say, 'Is he going right?' — until the speaker says, 'It is like . . .' — and then they listen eagerly for what it is like; and when some apt illustration is thrown out before them, there is a sense of relief, as though they said, 'Yes, he is right.' "*

The speaker, novelist, and playwright all have similar problems of preparation. Each has an idea he would like to convey. The problem is to paint it in impressive word pictures. The technique is described by an expert: "If there is one fact that we have grown to understand thoroughly and accept, it is the fact that we have nothing to understand with except our own experiences — the seeing and hearing and smelling and tasting and touching that we have done; the fearing and hoping and hating and loving that has happened in us; the intellectual and spiritual reactions that have resulted; and the assumptions, understandings, prides, prejudices, hypocrisies, fervors, foolishnesses, and faiths that have thereby been precipitated in us like crystals in a chemist's test tube.

"We are all, therefore, quite ready to nod our heads in agreement over statements that we read in terms of mental conceptions made out of this accumulated experience, just as a child builds castles from its wooden blocks.

---

* *Yale Lectures on Preaching*, p. 158. J. B. Ford and Company, New York. 1872.

We are, in other words, agreed upon the character of our building material."*

In the Mind's Eye

Few of us have the genius to discover truth, but most of us can find a new and stimulating point of view. Using picture-creating devices, we add interest to our idea and power to our purpose. We tell the experiences of ourselves and others in the fascinating details of word pictures. As they flash in the mind's eye of the listener, they create sound in his mind's ear and arouse in him sensations of smell, touch, and taste. We describe the appearance of a thing; we explain the nature of a problem; and we give reasons and use emotional appeals to promote a course of action. Thus, it may be seen that speaking is a combination of narration, description, explanation, and argumentation or persuasion.

Light Up

What is meant by the term, *illustration?* The word is derived from the Latin *illustrare* which means *to light up, to brighten.* Because of this origin, Beecher got the idea that an illustration "is a window that lets in light." He might have added that it also "lets in heat"; for illustrations appeal deeply to the feelings and emotions as well as to the mind and intellect. A

*J. B. Kerfoot, *How to Read*, p. 150. Houghton Mifflin Company, Boston. 1916. Reprinted by permission.

speech without them would be like a house without windows — dull and stuffy.

In the sense in which we are using the term, illustration is a detailed example, either *imaginary* or *real*. Usually, it is a story of an incident which the speaker uses to clarify his point. It is narrative in form, with details in vivid description. The main characteristic of illustration is its pictorial quality.

Pain Is Personal

Louis Nizer, a noted after-dinner speaker, says that "In making an emotional appeal it is well to remember a weakness common to us all. We can't be shocked by mass horrors. Only the individual instance stirs us. Perhaps this is due to the inability of the human mind to convey more than one burden at a time to the heart. Or perhaps we shrink from unpleasantness and this restricts our absorption capacity.

"My own notion is that we feel that which is personal. Reference to an individual causes us to substitute our own person for that of the victim. Then there is an impact upon our emotions. We are stirred by our own plight. We are frightened. But if the reference is to ten thousand people, we cannot transform ourselves into a mass and consequently the experience doesn't touch us."*

What is true of the emotion of fright is also true of other emotions. We project ourselves into the illustration whether it be of love, loyalty, or hate. This fact is reflected in sales courses where the indispensability of illustration is stressed by stories of "verbal-proof," "success-failure," "for-

---

* Nizer, *op. cit.*, pp. 246-47.

instance," and "who-did-it." The illustration possesses powers of persuasion not to be found in any other medium.

What Holds Attention Determines Action

William James, great American psychologist, taught that "What holds attention determines action." Even in the most intellectual listeners, attention ebbs and flows. It is held at a high peak for only a few consecutive moments.

Most speakers today are talking to the *moving-picture mind.* Their listeners are accustomed to sound, color, and action. Their problem is largely one of securing and maintaining voluntary attention. This is the kind that is given automatically without forced concentration of mind or will.

Few people will muster the strength of mind to give any attention at all under circumstances of boredom. Involuntary attention is best given by all types of audiences when the materials partake of the qualities described in this chapter. Even illustrations may be stifling if they do not partake of these characteristics.

Illustrations Arouse Imagery

We have all heard the word *pioneer.* What does it mean? There are two ways of arriving at an understanding of what it means: (1) by firsthand experience or (2) through vicarious experiences. The dictionary definition is abstract and conveys meaning only as related to the reader's experiences.

Direct experience comes through the senses of seeing, hearing, feeling, tasting, and smelling. The indirect experiences are acquired through reading and listening to narratives, descriptions, explanations, and arguments.

Of this ability to create in others a vicarious experience John Ruskin said: "The greatest thing a human soul ever does in this world is to *see* something, and tell what he *saw* in a plain way. Hundreds of people can talk for one who thinks, but thousands can think for one who can see. To see clearly is poetry, prophecy, religion — all in one."

Blazing the Trail

The word *pioneer* means little or nothing to the person who has never blazed a trail or read or heard a vivid pioneering story. It means everything to the old-timer who has struggled to redeem a wilderness of sagebrush and ravine. Narratives about pioneering help us feel the burning plains, muscles straining to pull and push the rickety handcarts through dust and mud, torrential rains and freezing snows, tired brows moist and hot with sudden fevers.

Giants in the Earth

Pioneers become "Giants in the Earth" in the adventures of grandparents or in Rölvaag's story. In his epic, the pioneers are Per Hansa and Beret, his wife. They build sod huts, trade with nomadic Indians, snare wild ducks, struggle through blinding blizzards, and brood under the hurt of religious isolation.

To sharpen more keenly the reader's conception of pioneering, Rölvaag describes a grasshopper plague in words of striking imagery.

Imagery by Description

"Down by the creek the grazing cows had hoisted their tails straight in the air and run for the nearest shelter; and no sooner had the horses been turned loose, than they followed suit; man and beast alike were overcome by a nameless fear.

"And now from out the sky gushed down with cruel force a living, pulsating stream, striking the backs of the helpless folk like pebbles thrown by an unseen hand; but that which fell out of the heavens was not pebbles, nor raindrops, nor hail, for then it would have lain inanimate where it fell; this substance had no sooner fallen than it popped up again, crackling, and snapping — rose up and disappeared in the twinkling of an eye; it flared and flitted around them like light gone mad; it chirped and buzzed through the air; it snapped and hopped along the ground; the whole place was a weltering turmoil of raging little demons; if one looked for a moment into the wind, one saw nothing but glittering, lightning-like flashes — flashes that came and went, in the heart of a cloud made up of innumerable dark-brown clicking bodies!

". . . they would stoop down, dashing and spreading out like an angry flood, slicing and shearing, cutting with greedy teeth, laying waste every foot of the field they lighted in . . . .

"In one field they would cut the stalks, leaving the ground strewn with a green carpet of heads; in the next they might content themselves with shearing the beard — then the grain looked like shorn sheep with the ears gone. Nor were they at all fastidious; potatoes and vegetables of all kinds, barley and oats, wheat and rye — it made no difference; or a swarm of insects might light on a wagon box, and when it lifted again the box would be scarred by countless sharp teeth; at one place a fork with a handle of hickory might be standing in the ground, and after a few swarms had passed the surface of the handle would be rasped and chewed, a mass of loose slivers; somewhere else a garment might be laid out on the ground to dry — a swarm would light on it, and in a moment only shreds would be left; if the annihilating devils were in the proper mood, they would take anything and leave nothing."*

Imagery by Narration

From a pioneer diary comes the story of John Stucki crossing the plains as a boy:

"My brother John, who pushed at the back of our cart, used to tell how hungry he was all the time and how tired he got from pushing. He said he felt if he could just sit down for a few minutes he would feel so much better. But instead, Father would ask if he couldn't push a little harder.

"When we got that chunk of buffalo meat, Father put it in the handcart, saying we would save it for Sunday dinner. John said, 'I was so hungry, and the meat smelled

---

* O. E. Rölvaag, *Giants in the Earth*, pp. 342-52. Harper and Brothers Publishers, New York. 1927. Reprinted by permission.

so good to me while pushing at the handcart that I could not resist. I had a little pocket knife and with it I cut off a piece or two each half-day. Although I expected a severe whipping when Father found it out, I cut off many little pieces. I would chew them so long that they got white and perfectly tasteless.

"When Father came to get the meat, he asked me if I had been helping myself. I said, 'Yes, Father, I was so hungry I could not let it alone.' Instead of giving me a scolding or whipping, my father turned away and wiped tears from his eyes."[*]

Mind Sight

To see clearly, to hear completely, to feel sensitively, to smell sharply, and to taste zestfully, one needs to hearken to the plea of Helen Keller:

"I who am blind can give one hint to those who see: Use your eyes as if tomorrow you would be stricken blind. And the same method can be applied to the other senses. Hear the music of voices, the song of a bird, the mighty strains of an orchestra, as if you would be stricken deaf tomorrow. Touch each object as if tomorrow your tactile sense would fail. Smell the perfume of flowers, taste with relish each morsel, as if tomorrow you could never smell and taste again. Make the most of every sense; glory in all the facets of pleasure and beauty which the world reveals to you through the several means of contact which Nature provides. But of all the senses, I am sure that sight is the

---

[*] Lorin F. Wheelwright, editor, Source Book, Arts Division, Utah Centennial, from the "Journal of Mary Ann Hafen," p. C 16. Utah Centennial Commission, Salt Lake City. 1947.

most delightful."* For the public speaker who wishes to develop compelling illustrations, this advice by Helen Keller is priceless !

Be More Than Specific, Be Concrete

There is a tale about a missionary who preached to the natives of the Fiji Islands. He told them that although their sins were as scarlet, belief in Jesus would make them white as snow. The natives were unmoved. Blank, staring expressions remained upon their faces. The missionary was perplexed.

The next day he returned and said, "Although your sins be as red as blood, if you will live as Jesus tells you, they will become as white as the milk of the coconut." The wide grins and nodding heads told the missionary that this time the natives understood.

The missionary had been specific in using the term "snow," but he had not been concrete. Snow was an abstraction to the natives. They had never seen it or felt it, but the "milk of the coconut" was for them life-giving food.

Few speakers are able to make themselves interesting unless their materials are not only specific but also concrete. Concreteness is a quality of the senses which is direct and physical. The abstract pertains to such concepts as color apart from a sunset and honesty apart from an Abe Lincoln. It is a quality apart from any particular object.

If I Had Three Days To See, p. 12. Reprinted at the Utah School for the Deaf, Salt Lake City. 1939.

Whether a thing is concrete or abstract depends on the experience of each individual. If he has seen, heard, tasted, smelled, or touched, it is not only specific but to him concrete. If he has not, it is a thing of thought only. "Who is my neighbor?" is abstract — a thing of the mind — until there is a good Samaritan in my experience or a picture of one such as Jesus created.

Radio, motion picture, and television are increasing the amount of concreteness in our thinking. They are more efficient in sensory stimulation than most of the literature we read. Places, people, animals, and ideas connected with industry, government, science, art, and religion that were once but mere names are becoming tangible in our mind's grasp.

More Than A Name

Taj Mahal, Mount Everest, Maoris were once only names to the writer. They were specific but remote and unreal and consequently not concrete. Some friends brought pictures and tales of the mosque and mountain, and I went to New Zealand to live among the Maoris. The brownskinned natives, of course, are now most concrete to me because I was among them. The same process accounts for concreteness in all our thinking.

The words *gravitation, buoyancy, reformation* were once meaningless symbols to me. When I hear them now, in my mind's eye I see Newton and the falling apple, Archimedes in his bathtub, and Luther nailing his ninety-five theses on the door of Castle Church. The number and correctness of such pictures will determine the concreteness — the extent and accuracy of our knowledge of any subject. In the words of an eighteenth century scholar, "The more general the terms are, the picture is fainter; the more special they are, 'tis the brighter."*

✓ There are different degrees of what is specific. *Mammal* is more specific than *animal*, *dog* than *mammal*, *Lassie* than *dog*. *Residence* is more specific than *building*, *cottage* than *residence*, *factory* than *structure*, and *attic* than *storage-place*. In fact, there are nearly a score of words that designate various types of particular buildings which arouse clearer and more vivid imagery than the more general term, *building*.

Echo and Re-echo

Simple words are generally more concrete than those of many syllables. The reason has never been better stated than in the language of Beecher: "The words which, from the cradle to the grave, have been the vehicles of love, trust, praise, hope, joy, anger, and hate, are not simple words, but, like paper, are what they are by virtue of the thing written on them. He who uses mainly Anglo-Saxon vocabulary, giving preference to the idoms and phrases which are homely, will have a power which cannot be derived from any other use. As a phrase in a mountainous country, when roundly uttered, goes on repeating itself from peak to peak, running in alternate reverberations through the whole valley, so a truth runs through all the ranges of memory in the mind of the hearer. The words themselves, full of secret suggestion and echoes, multiply the meaning in the minds of men, and make it even more in the recipient than it was in the speaker."† Anglo-Saxon words such as

---

* Dr. George Campbell.
† Beecher, *op. cit.*, p. 230.

love, food, home, fire, and *kiss* are more concrete and have greater impact upon the emotions of an audience than words of Latin and French origin such as *affection, victuals, domicile, conflagration,* and *osculation.*

Do Children Understand ?

One of American's greatest salesmen, John E. Kennedy, attributed much of his amazing success to the fact that he phrased his sales talks in "primer thought forms." Before giving his sales presentations to his prospects, Mr. Kennedy tried them out on youngsters of eighth grade school age. If he detected puzzled expressions on the faces of these youthful listeners, he would find out what was being misunderstood and why.* As the writer has listened to speeches couched in abstract, general, and difficult language, or a talk that bristled with technical and specialized terms, he has thought how wise we would all be if, in talking to lay and non-professional people, we would apply the sound advice of John E. Kennedy.

The Factors of Interestingness

Let us now summarize the value of concrete illustration by answering the question: "How can the attention of the audience be captured and held?" Phillips gave us an accurate guide nearly a half century ago. He called the material that secures and grips attention "The Factors of Interestingness."† Here they are:

Vital. Everyone is interested in living. The listener is concerned with his life, health, success, and happiness.

---

* Charles B. Roth, *Secrets of Closing Sales,* p. 13. Prentice-Hall, Inc., New York. 1940. Reprinted by permission.

† Arthur Edward Phillips, *Effective Speaking,* pp. 120-126. The Newton Company, Chicago. 1938. Reprinted by permission.

His primary interests have been defined as self-preservation, affections, power, property, and reputation.

Unusual. We are fascinated by things that are strange, fanciful, and unfamiliar. "What's new?" is the question we ask to secure information about strange peoples, lands, animals, discoveries, and odd occurrences.

Uncertain. This appeal arouses our curiosity about the outcome or the solution to a problem. There is a strong element of suspense in it. "How will it be settled?" we demand to know.

Similar. We feel comfortable and possess a sense of importance when we are near objects and situations with which we are familiar. Like attracts like.

Antagonistic. The listener's ear is always turned to conflict whether in people or things. Physical struggles — fights, feuds, hunts, or contests, floods or devastating winds; and intellectual grappling in debates or disputes — all glue the listener's ears to his mental arena.

Animate. Listeners are attracted to people and things that abound with vitality and activity. Materials that contain these qualities pack a punch and are a sure guarantee of audience interest. In a speaker enthusiasm is important.

Concrete. "To the average listener the philosopher is more interesting than philosophy; Christ's life more interesting than Christian life in the abstract; Solomon's Temple is more fascinating than the theory of architecture. Similarly with language. 'The sword' arrests the attention more than 'conflict,' 'the ballot' more than 'exercising the right of franchise.' "*

---

* Phillips, *op. cit.*, p. 126.

An illustration makes the point of the speech clearer and more vivid.

It possesses great power of emphasis.

It constitutes evidence and proof.

It sustains audience interest.

It stirs the imagination.

It aids the memory of both speaker and listener.

It presents controversial points of view in a less obvious manner.

It puts an idea over tactfully.

It gives intervals of enjoyment and relaxation.

It lends variety to the speech.

It ornaments the speech and enhances its style.*

No other material will reward the user so richly!

Caution: Prevent Glare

The words of Bishop Paul B. Kern should serve as a guide in the use of illustration: "The window shades are drawn and the room is dark. One shade is lifted and light streams in. Another shade is raised and through the window more light comes in. The third is lifted and the room is completely flooded with sunshine. This, my young friends, is what illustrations will do to your sermons. But there is one consideration you must bear in mind; after the room is well-lighted, the added effect of one or two more windows means little or nothing, except glare."

---

* Beecher, *op. cit.,* pp. 154-175.

Do not give an example or tell a story just for the sake of telling a story or merely because you think it will be interesting or that you have found or heard a good one. Do not tell a joke for the sole purpose of getting a laugh or to amuse. "That reminds me of a story" is the device so often used to drag one in for no good reason at all and is largely responsible for the groans when those trite words are heard. Properly used to drive home an idea, illustrations are effective tools.

Remember these rules in the use of illustration:

1. Do not over-illustrate.
2. Choose only the details that are necessary to create the picture.
3. Make certain the illustration is relevant to your speech purpose.
4. Keep the illustration new and fresh.

A Final Word by Lincoln

"I believe I have the popular reputation of being a storyteller, but I do not deserve the name in its general sense; for it is not the story itself but its purpose, or effect, that interests me. I often avoid a long and useless discussion by others or a laborious explanation on my own part by a short story that illustrates my point of view. So, too, the sharpness of a refusal or the edge of a rebuke may be blunted by an appropriate story, so as to save the wounded feeling and yet serve the purpose. No, I am not simply a storyteller, but storytelling as an emollient saves me much friction and distress."*

---

* To Colonel John D. Van Buren and others, June 26, 1863, in *The Lincoln Encyclopedia*, p. 347, compiled by Archer H. Shaw. The Macmillan Company, New York. 1950. Reprinted by permission.

CHAPTER VIII

SINEWS OF SPEECH

QUINTILIAN, in century one, B. C., wrote: "But an orator ought to be furnished, above all things, with an ample store of examples."* In the quaint English of the seventeenth century a brilliant scholar emphasized: "He that mindeth to perswade, must needes be well stored with examples. And therefore much are they to be commended, which searche Chronicles of all ages, and compare the state of our Elders with this present time."†

An Old Refrain

It's an old refrain! Ancient and modern thinkers affirm the importance of illustration in speech making.

This discussion continues the theme of the last chapter. It is something like taking a second look at a field of grain. One person sees the undulating waves of green turning to yellow. His viewpoint is aesthetic. Another sees the quality and value of the crop. His viewpoint is economic. In the previous chapter, illustration was described as a powerful tool capable of teaching more effectively than any other known device, because of its sensory imagery and its intensely personal appeal. There we discussed what illustration does to the listener. In this chapter we are looking at the importance of illustrations from another viewpoint. Here our purpose is to understand the various kinds of illustration useful to the speaker.

---

* *Institutes of Oratory*, II, 414. George Bell and Sons, New York. 1892.

† Thomas Wilson, *Arte of Rhetorique*, p. 190, Clarendon Press. Oxford, 1909.

Kinds of Illustration

Just as the first sentence in the recipe for cooking wild turkey is, "First catch your turkey," so the first step toward illustrating your talk is to find your illustrations. These may be classified as stories — factual or imaginary — anecdotes and jokes, fables, parables, and analogies. These types are narrative and descriptive. In addition there are illustrations where the narrative element may be present but not necessarily so. These forms are statistics, facts, quotation, testimony, restatement, specific example, explanation, and cumulation.* Comparison is inherent in all illustration.

Such materials may rightly be called the sinews of speech. They meet the specifications of a sinew as defined by Webster: "That which supplies strength or power, or in which the main strength, power, or support subsists."

The Human Interest Story

Stories about people, obscure or famous; or about things and events, humanly applied, strike the mind with great impact.

Of nearly four hundred articles that appeared in a small-town newspaper, 378 were about people: their loves, children, neighbors, pets, and activities. They were stories about the child lost in the snake-infested woods, the dog that struggled across a continent to find its young master, the well-digger entombed by his own excavation, the scientist who refused to empty his waste basket because it would

---

* See discussion of Chicago Round Table, Chapter XIII, for examples of many kinds of illustrations. See Chapter XV for discussion of testimony and quotation.

disturb a litter of new-born mice, and a king who abdicated his throne to marry a girl of the people.

In these human interest stories, we feed the same hunger that is satisfied in our children by the "Three Bears," "Tom Thumb," "Cinderella," and "Jack and the Beanstalk." Such stories may be pure fiction but when skilfully used, illustrate a point, and can have an appeal to the listener that is unrivaled.

Look for them in your own life and in the experiences of those about you. Seek them while you travel. Be alert for them as you read biography or history. Keep a sharp lookout as you scan the magazines and newspapers, Alertness and diligence are the price you pay for the possession of these precious speech materials.

Imaginary Illustration

An imaginary story or narrative supposes an incident in which certain things take place. If you do not have at hand an illustration that really has happened, you can "suppose" one.* The details should be consistent with truth and might actually occur. Lincoln, in explaining why slavery should be prohibited in the territories, used an imaginary illustration that brought the idea before his listeners with great force:

"If I saw a venomous snake crawling in the road, any man would say I might seize the nearest stick and kill it; but if I found that snake in bed with my children, that would be another question. I might hurt the children more than the snake, and it might bite them. Much more, if I

---

* See "Don't Die on Third," p. 132; "Emerson is Right," p. 137, for examples of factual illustrations.

found it in bed with my neighbor's children, and I had bound myself by a solemn compact not to meddle with his children under any circumstances, it would become me to let that particular mode of getting rid of the gentleman alone.

"But if there was a bed newly made up, to which the children were to be taken, and it was proposed to take a batch of young snakes and put them there with them, I take it no man would say there was any question how I ought to decide.

"That is just the case. The new territories are the newly-made bed to which our children are to go, and it lies with the nation to say whether they shall have snakes mixed up with them or not. It does not seem as if there could be much hesitation of what our policy should be."*

The Anecdote or Joke

The anecdote is often but not always a humorous story. It is a personal incident or bit of biography. Good taste demands that it not be of the back alley or washroom variety. For effectiveness it must always be appropriate to the point and the occasion.

The ability to tell an anecdote is a *must* for a versatile speaker just as a bit of humor is a *must* for most audiences. Humor takes monotony and dullness out of a speech. An anecdote generally is not real proof, but it may be the most powerful way in the world to make an idea either lucid or absurd.

---

* Speech, New Haven, Conn., March 6, 1860 in *The Lincoln Encyclopedia*, p. 328, compiled by Archer H. Shaw. The Macmillan Company, New York. 1950. Reprinted by permission.

The use of humor is something to develop. Scores of apparently humorless individuals have become adept in this important art.

Bennet Cerf is one of the world's foremost collectors of the humorous anecdote. He emphasized in a recent lecture that humor is becoming one of the most enjoyed of all American commodities. He said that the "insult joke" was not the kind in which to indulge. It is the humor of character that leaves the listener with a good feeling and a glow around the heart.

Mr. Cerf quoted the journalist, James Gordon Bennett, as saying that humor in the form of the joke or funny story does more for the mental health of the people than most of the sermons preached during the week. Mr. Cerf further declared that Danny Kaye, fun maker supreme, during a recent visit to England, had revealed the gentle, kindly, human quality of the American character, and that he had done more to promote good feeling between the nations than a hundred statesmen.

In its officer-training program, the Army stressed that "A sense of humor is one of the greatest assets to the speaker, and is evidenced by his manner as well as by his words. A sense of humor is never inconsistent with seriousness; it is essentially a mark of mental balance, for it is in reality an appreciation of relative values."*

A lecturer pointed out to a group of young men soon to enter professional life that "Humor is the salt of personality. Its presence is an evidence of good nature, of an appreciation of the real values of life, and a lack of tenseness.

* *Basic Field Manual Military Training*, FM 21-5, p. 43. Prepared under direction of Chief of Staff. U. S. Printing Office, Washington, D. C. 1941.

It is the most effective means of easing a difficult situation. Here it is important to differentiate between wit and humor; wit is of the mind, humor is of the heart."*

Sharpen the Point

Observe how this preacher uses a humorous anecdote to point up his idea and give his sermon a change of pace:

"You have become intimately aware of God's watchful care and the peace he can put in a man's heart. There is a fatal tendency in human nature to forget God when the crisis is removed.

"A friend of mine, an old Navy chaplain, tells of a terrible storm a couple of years ago; a storm so severe that even old seamen were scared. After it was all over an old salt-crusted sailor said, 'Chaplain, I sure did pray during that blow. I'm not a praying man, but I prayed hard that time.'

" 'What did you say in your prayer?' asked the chaplain.

" 'Oh,' replied the sailor, 'I said, 'Lord, you know that I have not asked you for anything for fifteen years, and if you'll get me out of this storm alive, I won't bother you again for another fifteen years!'

"This sailor is not the only one like that. We are going to need spiritual help in the

---

* Charles R. Gow, *Foundations for Human Engineering.* p. 173. The Macmillan Company, New York. 1930. Reprinted by permission.

days ahead, so if you have been praying each day, keep it
up; if you have been reading your Bible, keep at it; if, like
many families, you have been having family prayer, make
it a permanent thing in your household."*

The best humor is original and spontaneous and fits
the situation to which it is applied with nice exactness. The
foregoing anecdote is an excellent example. The story came
from the speaker's circle of acquaintances, as should yours,
if possible. Remember, a story going the "rounds" may be
so often repeated that its effectiveness is destroyed. The
"cracker" line was correctly worded. The rest depended
upon the skilful telling.

The Fable

Instead of dealing with people, as does the anecdote,
the fable personifies animals and inanimate objects. In
their actions we see more clearly the foibles of man.

Fables reveal vivid, efficient techniques of sharpening
a point. For many speakers, who tend to become wordy
in their storytelling, the fable could serve as a model of
terseness and economy in the use of concrete language.

There is much wisdom in fables awaiting discovery by
the alert speaker. Note how the following fable illustrates
an idea. Collections of fables offer many others as choice
as this.

"A jar of honey having been upset in a housekeeper's
room, a number of flies were attracted by its sweetness.
Placing their feet in it, they ate greedily. Their feet, how-

---

* Dr. Norman Vincent Peale, "How to Live in Peacetime," in *Think*. Feb-
ruary, 1946, p. 32. Reprinted by permission.

ever, became so smeared with honey that they could not use their wings, nor release themselves, and were suffocated. Just as they were expiring, they exclaimed: 'Oh, foolish creatures that we are, for the sake of a little pleasure we have destroyed ourselves.' "*

The Parable

The parable, too, has the power to turn "ears into eyes." It is a short, fictitious narrative from which a moral or spiritual truth is drawn.

Here is an example: "As Cannon Bell, of the University of Chicago, puts it, 'A Christian is not merely meant to be good in the sense that he is 'not bad,' but also good for something, good to help . . . .' Then, he mentions the parable of the wise and foolish virgins who went out to meet the bridegroom and to light his way. They slept, meanwhile, and their lamps went out. Five of them, having brought extra oil, filled their lamps. The other five had none and were obliged to go out and shop for more. While they were gone, the bridegroom came. He entered the temple and the doors were shut. The five heedless girls were barred. 'Why?' Cannon Bell asks. 'Why were they excluded from the bridal feast, which, in the story, is symbolic of heaven? Because of some evil they had done? There is no record of it — No, they had a piece of work to do in the name of Christ, the bridegroom. They were not prepared to do it. They left it undone!' "†

In this instance, the parable was not directly quoted, but its main points were aptly fitted to the idea of the speech.

---

* "The Flies and the Honey Pot," in the *Fables of Aesop*.
† John Ellis Large, "What is Man?" in *Vital Speeches*, Vol. XV, Number 24.

The Analogy

There are several types of comparison, but the one you are likely to use most often is the analogy. This kind of illustration is based on the theory that because two things are alike in several fundamental particulars, they will also be alike in other unknown and important details. It utilizes the technique of associating the unknown with the known.

Vash Young's Factory

In the following example, Vash Young compares himself with a factory: " 'Suppose you owned a factory,' I said to myself, 'would you manufacture only stuff that you do not want, do not need and cannot use to advantage? Would you deliberately operate your factory in such a way as to make it definitely harmful to you, the owner? Well, then, consider that you do own a factory, a thought factory. It is inside you, and you are both owner and superintendent. Also night watchman and everything else. Nothing can happen in that factory without your approval. Nothing can go into it, neither raw materials nor partly manufactured goods, except on your permission. Nothing can come out of it except the products that you yourself design.

" 'A thought factory! That's what you have inside you,' I said to myself, 'and you have turned it into a producer of junk. Take a look at your products. Fear, worry, impatience, anger, doubt. Are you proud of them? Can you expect other people to welcome such goods as you are manufacturing? Not a bit of it! Your factory is a menace to yourself and a nuisance to others.' ' "*

---

* Vash Young. *A Fortune to Share*, pp. 46-47. The Bobbs-Merrill Company, Inc., Indianapolis. 1931. Reprinted by permission.

Lincoln used a similar device in explaining his *position* to his critics during the Civil War. The newspapers were full of the feats of Blondin, a well-known tightrope walker. Lincoln made an impressive statement of his harrowing position by comparing it with the familiar hazards of Blondin:

"Gentlemen, I want you to suppose a case for a moment. Suppose that all the property you were worth was in gold, and you had put it in the hands of Blondin, the famous rope-walker, to carry across the Niagara Falls on a tight rope. Would you shake the rope while he was passing over it, or keep shouting to him, 'Blondin, stoop a little more! Go a little faster!' No, I am sure you would not. You would hold your breath as well as your tongue, and keep your hands off until he was safely over.

"Now, the government is in the same situation. It is carrying an immense weight across a stormy ocean. Untold treasures are in its hands. It is doing the best it can. Don't badger it! Just keep still, and it will get you safely over."

Lincoln used the words "suppose a case." They express a fundamental principle of analogy. He introduced his comparison smoothly and applied it to his appeal.

Figures, Facts, and Statistics

Figures and facts alone do not constitute statistics, especially when without relationship to a specific problem or question. If I say that butter is now higher than it has been at any time in history, I am stating a fact, provided my statement is true. If I continue by saying that butter is now seventy-five cents a pound, I am stating a figure and a fact.

Study the skill with which a Chamber of Commerce bulletin dramatizes statistics in a colorful story about Ted Williams and Babe Ruth:

"Ted Williams, Boston Red Sox Slugger, is being paid $125,000 this year for his services; Babe Ruth was paid $80,000 in 1931. After Uncle Sam collects from Mr. Williams he will have a net of $62,000, while Babe Ruth kept $68,000 of his $80,000. Mr. Williams will be able to buy with his money 57% of what Babe Ruth could buy with his money in 1931. If Ted Williams were to have as much buying power as Babe Ruth had, his salary would have to be $327,451."

Specific Example

Specific example* is an actual instance that is used to support a general idea. It may either merely mention a name, date, place, or incident or it may be a lengthy description or narrative.

---

* See "The Time is Now," p. 117, and "The Typical Dutchman," p. 174, for use of specific examples.

Explanation

You have likely noticed in many of the examples that have been cited that there has been a considerable amount of explanation. This device makes clear the relationship between the illustration and the idea it reinforces. It clarifies terms or meanings that may be obscure. Explanation requires skill. It enables the speaker to introduce an idea smoothly, to clarify a point, and to bind the thoughts that belong together.

In the following example, the speaker used explanation to introduce the "little prayer." After quoting the prayer, he used explanation again to make certain that the audience understood his interpretation of its meaning:

"There is a little prayer with which many of you no doubt are familiar; it provides a good formula for reasoning and may help you when faced with difficult decisions. The prayer goes as follows:

" 'Oh, Lord, give me strength and courage to try to change those things which should be changed for the benefit of mankind. Give me serenity and peace of mind to accept those things which cannot be changed. And give me the judgment and intelligence to know the difference.'

"You will note that this prayer has a significant factor in it which makes it far from simple, and that is the asking for divine guidance for intelligence to know the difference between what can and what cannot be changed."*

---

* James H. Halsey, "The Three R's of Higher Education," in *Vital Speeches*, Volume XV, Number 1.

Restatement and Cumulation

In the development of the specific purpose, the speaker should arrange his facts, illustrations, and explanations in such a way as to achieve weight of evidence by a "heaping up" of materials on the basic ideas of his speech. This device is known as *restatement* or *cumulation*.* Its method is to say the same thing over and over again, but to say it in different ways.

Variation in content keeps the idea fresh and sustains interest. Yet the abundance of materials adds the weight and force necessary to focus the mind upon the aim of the speech.

Repetition

Repetition is the expression of the same thought in identical language and may be used in hammering home a slogan or speech theme. Care should be taken lest it become tiresome.

Visual Aids

Visible materials sometimes do a better job of getting an idea across than any other means. They include use of blackboard, diagrams, maps, charts, pictures, cartoons, demonstrations, and the actual things about which you are to speak. These materials, to be *aids to vision*, above all things, must be shown in such a way as to be clearly seen by the entire audience. Small items should be enlarged by photography, photo projection, or drawing.

---

* See "The Time is Now" for examples of restatement and cumulation, p. 117.

Tested Interest Values

The importance of examples as sinews of speech is emphasized by this prescription; notice how dependent you are upon an ample store of illustration:

"Let us imagine that a speaker wanted to do something unusual: that is, instead of talking in terms of tradition, talk so that the audience wanted to listen. What would he do?

"1. He would slip in a personal experience or two. He would unashamedly tell of some conversation, experience, happening, that he knows about directly.

"2. He will consciously weave into his talk a concrete example, illustration, or incident which dares to get down to cases. As a matter of fact he will see to it that he says, 'For example," at least once every five minutes. Better yet, he will let the case make the point.

"3. He will explain as many ideas as possible with a comparison or analogy. 'The thing I'm talking about is like . . . ,' 'It is the same as . . . .'

"4. He will show pictures, diagrams, models, or objects so as to help the audience see what he is talking about. The popularity of the chalk-talk, the slide film show, and the actual demonstration over the straight speech is evidence that audiences find it easier to pay attention when the speaker uses visual materials.

"5. He will make certain that his speech is studded with moments of humor. . . . Note that the sentence says *moments* of humor. It says nothing about the gag man's professional effort to keep an audience roaring continuously. If in a twenty-minute talk a speaker unbends three times, say, for twenty seconds each time, that would almost be enough.

"Forget about belly laughs. If your effort brings just the shadow of a smile, that means the man is listening again. In short, a dash of humor serves as a kind of quick relief, a bit of first aid for a wearying spirit. . . .

"Be sure that you *know* the quip or story. There is much evidence that when the attempt at humor fails, the speaker was not in complete control of the material. Tell the story a dozen times to yourself or to anyone who will listen.

"Here is a way to test the interest value of a speech. If more than half of it is taken up with these five kinds of content materials [personal experience, concrete illustration, analogy, visual aids, and humor], the odds favor its 'listenability.' If three-quarters, the speech cannot miss. If less than one-quarter, the speaker might just as well have stayed home."*

Declared a Harvard scholar of a century ago: "Plan beforehand for one good fact and one good illustration under each head of your speech."†

* Irving J. Lee, "Why Don't You Give Interesting Speeches?" in *Oral Hygiene*, January, 1947, pp. 65-66. Reprinted by permission.

† Thomas Wentworth Higginson, "Hints on Speech Making," in *Modern Eloquence*, II, XX. Lincoln Scholarship Fund Edition. 1928.

CHAPTER IX

A SALUTE TO GENERAL PURPOSE

DWIGHT MORROW, distinguished ambassador to Mexico, was traveling on a train. Unable to find his ticket, he was embarrassed. The conductor recognized him and, observing his anxiety, reassured him by saying, "Don't worry, Mr. Morrow; I'm certain you have your ticket. When you find it, mail it to the company." "Worry be hanged," exploded Morrow, "if I don't find the ticket, I won't know where I'm going."

Too Many Speakers Lose Their Tickets

Speakers too frequently find themselves in Mr. Morrow's predicament. They forget that a speech is like a journey and must have a destination. Setting out for New Orleans, the verbal wanderer somehow ends up in Seattle. The effect such meandering has upon an audience is described by a Nebraska farmer who stepped into the town hall to hear the visiting spellbinder. As he sauntered outside for a bit of fresh air, a neighbor asked, "Jim, what's he a-talkin' about?" "I don't know," came the quick reply; "he ain't said."

What's he a-talkin about?

A Speech Is Like a Hunter's Gun

Without a goal a speech fails. The speaker has merely occupied time to enjoy hearing the sound of his own voice. He probably has insulted the intelligence of his audience and has proved himself to be a bore. To answer the question of the Nebraska farmer: "What's he a-talkin' about, Jim?" the speaker must have a target, take aim, and call his shot.

Blazing away at a hillside brings down no game. The effective speaker must aim straight and fire ammunition of a calibre to penetrate his objective. Henry Ward Beecher emphasized the importance of formulating a purpose when he said: "A speech is not like a Chinese firecracker, to be fired off for the noise it makes. It is a hunter's gun, and at every discharge the speaker should look to see his game fall."

Fire Power

"Did you ever watch a circus crew driving stakes for the big tent? First the stake is placed in the right position, and then four or five men with sledge hammers beat a 'rat-tat-tat-tat-tat!' upon its head until it is securely driven into the ground.

"Did you ever see a gunner's squad load a piece of artillery? First the shell is pushed into the breech, and then behind it is packed the charge of explosive.

"Did you ever see a football player make a punt? He holds the football in the right way; drops it, then a dull 'pug' tells the story of the force behind the kick that sends the ball sailing down the field.

"What is the point? Just this — *in every case, two things are needed: first, an objective to drive home, and second, power to drive it.*

"Just so with the speaker. He wants to drive home his thoughts so that, like the shell, they will burst through barriers of indifference and force their way into the consciousness of the hearer. He wants to drive home his ideas so thoroughly that they will hold, like the tent stakes, no matter how hard the winds of forgetfulness may blow. If he is to do this, *he must have a worth-while idea to drive home, and ammunition enough to drive it to its mark.*"*

So What ?

This vivid quotation from Monroe and Lull dramatizes the relationship between speech purpose and supporting material. In itself, it is an example of how to avoid the abstract, the unsupported statement, and the mere assertion of opinion. It demonstrates how to compel an audience to listen, how to amplify an idea by painting word pictures on a canvas of analogy. Quotations, anecdotes, statistics, poems, and additional explanation might have been used had the requirements of the idea and audience demanded.

General Purpose — Molder of Strategy

In effect, the foregoing quotation is a short speech whose purposes may be defined as general and specific. In this instance the general purpose is *to inform.* The specific purpose is to show that a speaker must have a worth-while idea and enough ammunition to drive it home. When planning a speech on any subject, the speaker must formulate his *general* purpose before phrasing the *specific* purpose or central idea.

The general purpose may be one or a combination of reactions the speaker wants from his audience. They are five in number: *to inform, to impress, to convince, to persuade,* and *to entertain.*

---

* Alan H. Monroe and Paul E. Lull, *Projects in Speech for a Foundation Course*, p. 39. D. C. Heath and Company, Chicago. 1931. Reprinted by permission.

To Inform

Perhaps the most common of all the general purposes is *to inform*. It succeeds when the hearer says, "I see," "I understand," "I comprehend." It seeks to instruct, to explain, to clarify facts, to increase knowledge. You inform when you explain the principles of your religion. You inform when you tell someone how to build a model airplane, how to solve a problem, how to rear a child, or how to drive an automobile. Clarity of understanding is the objective. The informative speech is composed primarily of facts, definitions, concrete examples, and statistics. It becomes clear when the speaker uses the right words and visual aids, such as charts, pictures, graphs, maps, diagrams, specimens, and models.

The following paragraph from a speech commemorating the birthday of Thomas A. Edison has as its general purpose to inform. The specific purpose makes clear how electric light can dispel the darkness of the mind.

"I remember when I was a small boy on the East Side of New York. The only light we had was an open gaslight. Then came the Welsbach mantel, and we were all excited by the great improvement. Then, one day, we saw electric lights all about us. We were amazed at this wonder. But soon we took that in our stride. We even complained that the streets were still lighted by gaslight. We demanded streets lighted by electricity.

"In the many years I lived in China, I saw literally millions of men and women who had never seen an electric light. The only artificial lighting they had — as a matter of fact, still have — is an oil lamp or a candle; most of them go to bed with the dark and rise at dawn. They are limited in their reading, their learning, their leisure by the darkness, and what I say of peasant and village life in China was equally true of Siberia in very recent years. It is true of much of this world. They live in darkness."*

To Impress

If, in addition to giving information, the speech portrays the idea so vividly that the listener *feels* as well as sees, its general purpose is *to impress*. When this is the purpose, the speaker generally talks about points of view and attitudes already accepted by his listeners; for example, he gives a "pep" talk at a sales meeting; he speaks a eulogy at a funeral; or he extols the patriots on the Fourth of July. He wants to heighten and deepen the pull of basic convictions and ideals. His goal is to make them more significant by vivid words and illustrations.

An American statesman in the following eulogy to mothers seeks *to impress* as his general purpose. His specific purpose is to make his listeners feel that mothers are a fount of virtue and an inspiration to their children.

---

* George E. Sokolsky, "Lincoln and Edison," in *Vital Speeches*, Volume XV, Number 12.

"And, it seems to me that much and great good could be accomplished in the direction of lasting peace if the nations of the world ever keep before them the simple, wise, and just advice that mothers of men impart to their little ones at their knees. As I say this, I recall the advice which the mother of Andrew Jackson, a great leader and the seventh President of the United States, gave to him shortly before she died. It impressed me so deeply that I have never forgotten it. She said:

" 'Andrew, if I should not see you again, I wish you to remember and treasure up some things I have already said to you: In this world you will have to make your own way. To do that you must have friends. You can make friends by being honest, and you can keep them by being steadfast.

" 'You must keep in mind that friends worth having will in the long run expect as much from you as they give to you. To forget an obligation or be ungrateful for a kindness is a base crime — not merely a fault or a sin, but an actual crime. Men guilty of it sooner or later must suffer the penalty.

" 'In personal conduct be always polite but never obsequious. None will respect you more than you respect yourself. Avoid quarrels as long as you can without yielding to imposition. But sustain your manhood always. Never bring a suit in law for assault and battery or for defamation. The law affords no remedy for such outrages that can satisfy the feelings of a true man. Never wound the feelings of others. Never brook wanton outrage upon your own feelings.   If you ever have to vindicate your feelings or defend your honor, do it calmly. If angry at first, wait till your wrath cools off before you proceed.'

"These words were repeated by General Jackson on his birthday, March 15, 1815, at New Orleans, to three members of his military family. 'Gentlemen,' said General Jackson, 'I wish she could have lived to see this day. There never was a woman like her. She was gentle as a dove and as brave as a lioness. Her last words have been the law of my life.' "*

To Convince

To persuade, the speaker must first convince. His immediate goal is to secure an open mind, and his ultimate objective is to obtain a decision or a mind that is again "made up." To induce belief or to convince is primarily intellectual in appeal. Speakers may strive for convictions on many issues; for example, the city manager plan, the building of a church, the importance of learning to speak, or the value of an education. The speech to convince attempts to prove something and is composed of argument supported with logic, facts, figures, examples, and opinions.

Professor Lionel Crocker, in the following talk, seeks to convince a graduating class of seniors that they must learn to speak if they are to attain eminent positions in public service:

"Russell Conwell declared in his famous lecture, 'Acres of Diamonds,' that if you want to be an orator as a man, you speak your piece as a boy. . . . How badly society needs the public speaker! Social control is exercised through personality, and personality is expressed through the written and spoken word. Through expression we help to discover the truth . . . . I wish to impress upon you the necessity of

---

* James A. Farley, "Our Mothers," in *Vital Speeches*, Volume XV, Number 15.

skill in speaking in the make-up of the leader in society today. Think of any of the dozen or so personalities who are before the world today, and after some reflection you will admit that they rose to their position of leadership largely because they could speak . . . .

"Did it ever occur to you that Abraham Lincoln became president of the United States because of his ability to find the truth through public discussion? Abraham Lincoln was not a governor of a state as were Roosevelt, Wilson, and Harding. Abraham Lincoln achieved the necessary prominence to make him President of the United States through his debates with Douglas and his Cooper Institute Address. Two of the three greatest pieces of oratorical prose in the English language came from the lips of Abraham Lincoln. William Jennings Bryan has said, 'Lincoln's elevation to the Presidency would have been impossible without his oratory.'

"Henry Ward Beecner, through the power of the word, showed the ruling classes of England in the fall of 1863 how the masses felt about the question of slavery. The masses were disenfranchised; they could not vote; the newspapers were closed to them. The only way they could make their mass influence felt was through assembly. The only orator who was capable of conducting these mass meetings was the greatest ever to preach in America, Henry Ward Beecher.

"Both Lincoln and Beecher studied to improve themselves as public speakers. Lincoln studied William Scott's *Lessons in Elocution*. Beecher praised the instruction he received from his teacher, John Lovell, at Amherst.

"After taking this glance at these two examples of leadership through the spoken word may I point your attention to some of the great personalities of today and show how their skill in speaking contributed to that leadership.

"Last year I made a special study of Lowell Thomas. I found that Lowell Thomas did not achieve his prominence as a radio news reporter by accident. He was a teacher of public speaking at Kent College of Law in Chicago and later taught public speaking at Princeton University. How much he values his public speaking training and ability is revealed in this letter he wrote me:

" 'I could write volumes on the subject of my public speaking adventures. My friends seem to think that I have had more than my fair share of fun — jaunts around the world, expeditions to far countries, association with many of the world's leaders and glamorous figures and so on. Well, I owe it almost entirely to public speaking.

" 'As I look back on it now, if given the chance to do it all over again, and if obliged to choose between four years of college and two years of straight public speaking, I would take the latter because under the proper direction it could include most of what one gets from a four year Liberal Arts course, and then some. I can think of nothing that is more likely to add cubits to your stature than well-rounded training in public speaking, combined with plenty of practical experience.'"*

To Persuade

Persuasion translates conviction into a mode of action. The audience must respond in some definite, observable

---

* Lionel Crocker, "Leadership and the Spoken Word," in *Vital Speeches,* Volume VIII, Number 6.

manner. Action means *doing* and is the most difficult to achieve of all the general ends. Most persons do not act from caprice or chance. They must be moved.

Facts, logic, and examples may open the minds of the hostile; the friendly may nod in agreement; and the indifferent may be stimulated to sit up and listen; but interest and agreement are not enough. Although the individual listener may be convinced, there is no guarantee that he will act upon his conviction. The problem is to get him to *want* something for himself.

Evidence of this truth is on every hand. The individual may fight for democracy but seldom vote. He may know that liquor and tobacco are damaging to his health and continue to indulge heavily in both. He may believe that the teachings of Jesus are the most precious of all philosophy but do nothing to apply them in his life. He may accept the fact that to be in debt is to endanger his future but make no effort to live within his income. These are but a few of the convictions that he might be willing to accept and even fight for but actually do little to live for.

Here is a vivid statement by a contemporary speaker contrasting our lukewarm attitude toward democracy with the chauvinism of the Russians: "The situation resolves itself down to this. The Russians have the zeal but no truth; we have the truth but no zeal; they have the passion but no ideal; we have the ideals but no passion. Neither of us is right. They sin against the light; we sin against love."*

---

*From a radio talk entitled "Communism and the Revival of Passion," by Msgr. Fulton J. Sheen.

Motive Power Does It

The problem of the persuasive speaker is to create zeal for the truth, light, and ideals he wishes his listeners to accept. He must arouse and sharpen their intellectual, spiritual, and moral aspirations. He must stimulate the listeners' emotions so decisively that inertia will be overcome. To be reasonably successful, the speaker must be definite and specific in asking for the response he seeks. He must be confident and enthusiastic in his manner. These qualities are fundamental, but they are not enough.

Beyond this, the speaker must become expert in the use of the universal drives which motivate human behavior. Beecher stressed this requirement of the speaker when he said, "A man may know the Bible from Genesis to Revelation; he may know every theological treatise from the day of Augustine to the day of Dr. Taylor; and if he does not understand human nature, he is not fit to preach."*

Sounding the Depths

John Quincy Adams, sixth President of the United States, lectured at Harvard University about understanding the audience and the appeals to which it responds. Adams said: "By the power of imagination the orator undergoes a virtual transformation. He identifies himself either with the person, in whose behalf he would excite the sentiment of compassion, or with the antagonist, against whom he is to contend, or with the auditor, whom he is to convince or persuade. Of his client he learns what he most keenly feels; of the antagonist what he most seriously dreads; of

---

* *Yale Lectures on Preaching*, first series, p. 85. The Pilgrim Press, Boston. 1872.

the auditor what he most readily believes. He sounds the depths of every heart; he measures the compass of every mind; he explores the secret recesses of nature herself."*

The distinguished American historian, James Truslow Adams, declared: "In my opinion, man is an extraordinarily complex organism, subject to all sorts of motives — religion, money, pride, ambition, love of adventure, intellectual curiosity, sexual love, hate, and the others."†

Sad But True

Herbert Hoover points out that in appealing to the individual it is well to remember that man is primarily selfish. These are his words: "The inherited instincts of self-preservation, acquisitiveness, fear, kindness, hate, curiosity, desire for self-expression, for power, for adulation, that we carry over from a thousand generations must, for good or evil, be comprehended in a workable system embracing our accumulation of experiences and equipment. They may modify themselves with time — but in terms of generations. They differ in their urge upon different individuals. The dominant ones are selfish."‡

A Guide Through the Maze

H. D. Kitson, an authority in the field of salesmanship, groups these basic motives into three classifications:

"1. those which preserve the life and provide for the welfare of the individual; such as flight, pugnacity, hoarding, curiosity.

---

* *Lectures on Rhetoric and Oratory,* I, 382-83. Hilliard and Metcalf, Cambridge. 1810.

† "My Methods as a Historian," in the *Saturday Review of Literature* (June 30, 1934), X, 778.

‡ *American Individualism,* p. 15. Doubleday, Doran and Co., Inc., New York. 1922.

2. those which provide for the continuance of the race and family; such as mating, protection of home and young.

3. those which make for the welfare of the tribe or social unit; such as gregariousness, imitation.

Some of the acts belong to more than one class. . . . The division is convenient in general and may serve as a guide through the maze."*

Impelling Motives

Impelling motives is the term for those appeals that are best known to speakers. They "may be defined as man's spiritual, intellectual, moral, and material wants."† They are self-preservation, property, power, reputation, affections, sentiments, and tastes.

On every hand the man of today is besieged by the call of such appeals. How a speaker of another generation used some of these appeals should afford a bit of interesting variation. George Graham Vest was a lawyer in Missouri and a United States Senator in the last quarter of the nineteenth century. Judge John F. Dillon, after listening to him before the Eighth Circuit Court, said, "I have never heard so great a jury speech in my life." And his law partner states that Vest had no equal in the state as a popular speaker. Before the Johnson County Circuit Court in Missouri, Vest pleaded for "exemplary damages for the value of his client's favorite dog" with complete success. He drew "tears from the jury in the box and applause from the spectators, with a pathos and eloquence never to be forgotten by those who heard

* *The Mind of the Buyer*, pp. 147-48. The Macmillan Company, New York, 1921. Reprinted by permission.

† Arthur E. Phillips, *Effective Speaking*, p. 105. The Newton Company, Chicago. 1938.

him." Although the language is of another period and somewhat flowery, picture its effects in a dramatic setting. Study the appeals to sentiment, affection, and property made by the speech:

"Gentlemen of the Jury: The best human friend a man has in the world may turn against him and become his enemy. His son or daughter that he has reared with loving care may prove ungrateful. Those who are nearest and dearest to us, those whom we trust with our happiness and our good name may become traitors to their faith. The money that a man has he may lose. It flies away from him, perhaps, when he needs it most. A man's reputation may be sacrificed in a moment of ill-considered action. The people who are prone to fall on their knees to do us honor when success is with us may be the first to throw the stone of malice when failure settles its cloud upon our heads. The one absolutely unselfish friend that a man can have in this selfish world, the one that never deceives him, the one that never proves ungrateful and treacherous, is his dog.

"A man's dog stands by him in prosperity and in poverty, in health and in sickness. He will sleep on the cold ground where the wintry wind blows and the snow drifts fiercely, if only he may be near his master's side. He will kiss the hand that has no food to offer. He will lick the wounds and sores that come in encounter with the roughness of the world. He guards the sleep of his pauper master as if he were a prince. When all other friends desert, he remains. When riches take wings and reputation falls to pieces, he is as constant in his love as the sun in its journey through the heavens. If fortune drives the master forth, an outcast in the world, friendless and homeless, the faithful dog asks no higher privilege than that of accompanying, to guard against danger, to fight against his enemies, and when the last scene of all comes and death takes the master in its embrace and his body is laid away in the cold ground, no matter if all other friends pursue their way, there by the graveside may the noble dog be found, his head between his paws, his eyes sad but open in alert watchfulness, faithful and true even in death."*

This talk by Senator Vest illustrates two other factors in persuasive speech that the speaker should remember. One of these is the power of suggestion. Suggestion in its extreme form is hypnosis. It seeks the acceptance of an idea without logical consideration of its merits. If slogans and propositions are repeated often enough and forcibly enough, they are likely to be accepted without evidence. In his talk to the jury, Senator Vest reiterated in every conceivable way and with all his confidence, power, and personal prestige the faithfulness of the dog to his master. He used suggestion!

---

* "Eulogy on the Dog," in *Library of Southern Literature*, XII, 5575-92. The Martin and Hoyt Company, Atlanta, Georgia. 1907.

The second factor, one that has been often repeated, is the use of verbal pictures, words that carry compelling, vivid imagery. Study Vest's speech for this feature, and you will understand why the jury shed tears. A famous writer rightly said, "He who wants to persuade should put his trust, not in the right argument, but in the right word."*

To Entertain

The whole object of some speeches is to amuse and give pleasure. Humor in speaking, however, is a means of creating readiness in the listener to receive serious and thought-provoking ideas. In reality, entertainment is present in all successful speech making. It helps the audience remain relaxed, yet alert.

People enjoy a good cry as well as a laugh. The pleasure may stem from any well-told illustration or anecdote, whether funny or not. As has already been stressed, that material which is vital, unusual, uncertain, similar, antagonistic, animate, and concrete affords enjoyment.

Laughter creates good will. It makes the audience more responsive to suggestion from the speaker. Humor derives from dramatizing the peculiar traits of people, from exaggeration and understatement, from poking fun at conventional modes of conduct and false dignity.

Mark Twain Could Entertain

Incongruities in human nature and situations are conveyed to the listener through the *speaker's attitude and phrasing*. Nearly anyone with practice can relate his own experiences in a style similar to that of Mark Twain in his

---

* Joseph Conrad.

lecture on "The Sandwich Islands."* Here are several excerpts:

"In the rural districts the [Hawaiian] women wear a single loose gown. But the men don't. [Laughter] The men wear, . . . well, as a general thing, they wear . . . a smile, or a pair of spectacles, . . . or any little thing like that. [Laughter] But they are not proud. They don't seem to care for display. [Laughter] . . .

"They [the Hawaiians] are an odd sort of people. They can die whenever they want to. [Laughter] They don't mind dying any more than a jilted Frenchman does. When they take a notion to die, they die, and it doesn't make any difference whether there is anything the matter with them or not, and they can't be persuaded out of it. When one of them makes up his mind to die, he just lies down and is as certain to die as though he had all the doctors in the world hold of him! [Laughter] . . .

"These people love their puppies better than they love each other, and a puppy always has plenty to eat, even if the rest of the family must go hungry . . . . They feed him with their own hands, and fondle and pet and caress him, till he is a full-grown dog, and then they eat him. Now, I couldn't do that. [Laughter] I'd rather go hungry two days than eat an old friend that way. [Laughter] There's something sad about that. [Laughter] . . . Many a white citizen learns to throw aside his prejudices and eat of the dish. After all, it's our own American sausage with the mystery removed. [Laughter]"*

---

*Modern Eloquence, XIII, 134-37. Lincoln Scholarship Fund Edition. New York. 1928.

"Be at Rest"

The unexpected ending to an anecdote is one of the surest ways to evoke laughter; for example, two senior citizens of a small community decided to attend the graveside services of a friend. Having little to occupy their time, they set out to walk to the cemetery which was about three miles away. Pretty well tuckered out by the time they arrived, they sat down on a fallen tombstone on which was inscribed, "Be at Rest."

It occurred to one of them to ask, "How old be you, Henry?"

"Be eighty-one, come next month. How old be you, Ezra?"

"Be eighty-six next September."

"My land, Ezra," said Henry, with a twinkle in his eye, "it don't hardly seem like it'll pay you to walk home!"

In using humor, the speaker should enjoy a playful attitude with the audience but avoid laughing at his own stories. His voice and action must express the mood and substance of his material.

One Purpose Controls

The speaker may be required to inform and impress before he can persuade. Although several of the five general purposes may be present, one should largely control the kinds of material and appeals that build the speech.

Specific Purpose Completes the Goal

A speaker never appears before his listeners with only the general intention to inform or to persuade. He comes with a specific purpose in minde. He wants to persuade his audience to act in a definite and specific way or to understand some precise and well-defined information. The specific purpose is the exact proposition the speaker wants the audience to understand, feel, believe, perform, or enjoy.

If a speech is to be a hunter's gun with fire power enough to reach the speaker's objective, the idea must be driven home through constant repetition of the specific purpose.

Notice how Henry van Dyke repeats his *specific purpose* in this talk:

He said, "Let me etch the portrait of the typical Dutchman. Grant me but six strokes for the picture." Then followed the main ideas in support of the specific purpose. They, in turn, were amplified by examples, illustrations, poems, quotations, comparisons, and explanation.

Here are the main ideas:

"I. The typical Dutchman is an *honest* man.

II. The typical Dutchman is a *free* man.

III. The typical Dutchman is a *prudent* man.

IV. The typical Dutchman is a *devout* man.

V. The typical Dutchman is a *liberal* man.

VI. But one more stroke remains to be added to the picture. The typical Dutchman is a man of *few* words."*

Observe how this commencement speaker drives home his *specific purpose*, "The Time Is Now," through repetition.

---

* *Modern Eloquence*, III, 363-67. Lincoln Scholarship Fund Edition. New York. 1928.

The Time Is Now

"Youth is a time of dreaming, a time of long, long thoughts. It is a time of idealistic and generous impulse. Often the dream is of a distant day when the dreamer will work miracles. The difference between the dream of one person and the dream of another is less its content than in what the dreamer does about it.

"The great of this earth, measured by reputation and impact on events, are those who seek to translate the dream into instant reality, but who are not discouraged that progress is slower than vision. For them the time is now, not some remote tomorrow which, like a mirage, recedes as it is approached. So dream, yes, but be the kind of dreamer for whom the time for action is not some more favorable tomorrow, but for whom the time for action is now.

"Don't be intimidated by the fact of youth. Let history encourage you. Alexander the Great, a military hero at eighteen, began his efforts to conquer and control the earth at twenty. At his death at the age of thirty-three, he had exercised dominion over much of the civilized world of his day. For Alexander the time was now.

"Jeanne d'Arc, at nineteen, had completed her mission and embraced the immortality of martyrdom. Isaac Newton, at twenty-one, had contributed importantly to mathematics. At twenty-five he was honored with a professorship at Cambridge University.

"Alexander Hamilton, at eighteen, was famed as an orator for freedom's cause. At twenty he was a lieutenant colonel on George Washington's staff, and Washington's trusted confidential secretary. Lafayette, burning to help

France and deciding the best way to do so was weaken England by aiding the revolting American colonies, was a major general in Washington's army at nineteen.

"William Pitt, the younger, one of Britain's greatest statesmen, successfully sought election to Parliament at the age of twenty-one. He became Prime Minister before he was twenty-five.

"Winston Churchill, on the eve of going abroad as a foreign correspondent, though not yet twenty-one, gave a farewell dinner party for some of his youthful friends. He proposed a toast to 'Those yet under twenty-one who, in twenty years, will control the British Empire.'

"Henry Luce had already founded his journalistic empire when he was twenty-five. At twenty-nine, Earl Warren was deputy district attorney for the important county of Alameda. At thirty-one Harold Stassen was Governor of Minnesota.

"For each of this company of illustrious names, dreams were incitements to action. For each, the time was now."*

In Conclusion

The gist of the whole matter is summarized by Dr. Lyman Abbott, famous as an orator of another period:

"The man coming before an audience should ask himself this question, first, 'What is the object of this speech? What end is it to serve? What verdict is it to win? What result is it to accomplish?' [General purpose]

---

* Raymond G. McKelvey, "The Time Is Now!" in *Vital Speeches*, Volume XIV, Number 24.

"Secondly, he is to make up his own mind as to the central idea of his speech: 'What thought lodged in the mind of an auditor will best accomplish the desired result?' [Specific purpose.]

"Thirdly, he is to resolve 'this central thought into three or four propositions, the inforcement and illustration of which will serve to fasten in the minds of the hearers the central thought, and so secure the desired result.' [Main ideas]

"Fourthly, he must be ready with 'some illustrations or concrete statements of each one of these separate propositions.'

"Finally, this preparatory labor having been completed, the speaker, when he gets on his feet, should endeavor 'on these lines of thought, to win this result with his audience, exactly as one would endeavor to win assent from an individual,' speaking simply and conversationally, and 'rising into the oratorical only as the excitement of the occasion and the attention of the audience produces, spontaneously, the change.' "*

---

* Brander Matthews, "Four Ways of Delivering An Address," quoting Lyman Abbott, *Modern Eloquence*, I, xxxi. Lincoln Scholarship Fund Edition.

CHAPTER X

PLANNING A PLAN

PROBABLY the shortest address ever given on a public occasion was this one by President Abraham Lincoln at a flag-raising ceremony. He began and concluded his talk in one sentence: "The part assigned to me is to raise the flag, which, if there be no fault in the machinery, I will do, and when up, it will be for the people to keep it up."*

Such a talk would not, of course, require an outline. But when an outline was essential, Lincoln made one, as is shown in his preparation for a trial involving three sons, a grandson, their sisters and husbands. The issue was to decide to which faction a dying old man intended to leave certain lands and other belongings. Lincoln was the lawyer for the sons.

Lincoln's Outline

In preparing his remarks for the jury, Lincoln employed a method which is worthy of emulation by every speaker. After analyzing the occasion, the audience (jury in this case), and the subject, he laid out before him all of the material that he had been accumulating for the talk. He did not write a speech, but he set down fifteen pages of reasons why his clients should receive the property. Then, he organized the supporting facts,

* The Wit and Wisdom of Abraham Lincoln, p. 170, edited by H. Jack Lang. The World Publishing Company, New York. 1942.

testimonies, and examples. These were his materials which he refined into an outline by eliminating those things that were irrelevant or less important.

Lincoln's final outline* looked something like this:

AUDIENCE: Jury in Will Case.

GENERAL PURPOSE: To persuade.

SPECIFIC PURPOSE: To secure the benefits of the provisions of the will for my clients by establishing them as the rightful heirs.

Introduction

I. Give general remarks on the law of wills.

II. Answer particular points and objections made by other side.

A. See notes taken.

III. Settle definition of "sound mind and memory."

A. Read from authorities.

IV. Show the testator had such "sound mind and memory."

A. At time of making the will.

Discussion

I. Testator asked a doctor to write his will.

II. He gave a rational answer to a woman.

A. She had asserted he was too weak to make a will.

---

* Symbols, statement of purpose, division into introduction, discussion, and conclusion are by the author. Adapted from Carl Sandburg, *Abraham Lincoln, The Prairie Years*, Vol II, p. 319. Harcourt, Brace & Company, New York. 1926. Reprinted by permission.

III. He said his will was made.

    A. He had received the papers with which to make it.

        1. He got a roll of blank papers.

        2. He got a package of title paper.

IV. He first made provision for his wife.

    A. He provided that one son pay rent to his mother.

V. He made a decision as to what was to be done with home and place.

    A. He made a rational reply when one woman suggested she should have the house.

VI. His recollection of two persons he hated was lucid.

    A. This occurred on his deathbed.

VII. He was eager about his will.

    A. The night before it was made.

    B. On the day it was made.

    C. On the day after it was made.

Conclusion

I. The testator remained quiet until he died.

NOTE: Judge Stephen T. Logan (opposing counsel and one of the highest-paid lawyers in Illinois) resumes after dinner. He admonished jury to watch me *very* closely. He says some judges decide one way, and some another in will cases.

Lincoln's notes show that he used his outline to make clear the relationship of ideas and the sequence in which they should be presented to the jury. The note at the bottom indicates that it included any bit of information that would be helpful to the speaker.

From Lincoln's outline we can learn several fundamental principles: Analyze the audience in order to beam your material to their understanding and interests. State both your general and specific purpose. Divide the material into introduction (or beginning), body (or discussion), and conclusion (or ending), according to its function in the speech. Prepare the discussion first, then construct an appropriate introduction and conclusion. This sequence will help you shape the introduction and conclusion to fit the discussion.

Lincoln had more points in his talk than are required for most situations. Of course, he may have spoken for several hours to cover his case. The typical occasion limits the present-day speaker to twenty or thirty minutes and to not more than three or four main points.

See that each division of your talk performs its intended function. Observe that in Lincoln's introduction he handled all preliminary matters. Then he introduced the specific purpose of his speech which was, "Testator had sound mind and memory."

Outline Profile

Use symbols to show the relationship of ideas as portrayed in this outline on outlining:

I. Roman numerals are used in the discussion to designate the main ideas that support the specific purpose.

   A. Capital letters are used for the first subheads.

      1. Arabic numerals designate the next subordinate ideas.

         a. Then small letters are used.

(1) If another set is needed, Arabic numbers in parentheses are used next.

II. The marginal indentations for coordinate ideas must be carefully observed to avoid confusion.

A. The outline should be blocked as shown in the examples. Do not permit the contents to overlap adjacent margins.

B. For ready and easy use of the outline leave considerable white space on the page.

1. Key word outlines best provide this advantage.

III. Outlining should be used at all stages in the preparation.

A. The preliminary outlining may not be the final one.

I. Make an outline to get a first comprehensive view of your plan.

2. Keep refining the outline at every stage in the preparation.

a. This will keep you from going off on tangents.

b. This will help you keep out irrelevant materials.

c. This will enable you to look at your talk objectively.

(1) You will be able to see whether it is in appropriate order.

(2) You will be able to see whether your talk is well-balanced.

(3) You will be able to see whether it is coherent and unified or loosely put together.

(4) You will be able to see whether the main ideas are supported with a variety of fact, illustration, and explanation.

(5) You will be able to analyze discussion, introduction, and conclusion.

(6) You will be able to make certain that transitions are present in the speech.

Key Words

An outline consists of a series of words, phrases, or sentences arranged to show coordinate and subordinate relationships. The author of this volume prefers an outline of key words or list of words. Each word suggests a topic. The speech details are so familiar to the speaker that they are readily  supplied as he talks. The following is an example of a key word outline taken from a talk on speech delivery:

    I. Directness

        A. Definition

           1. Dictionary

           2. Speech authority

        B. Mothers' Club

        C. Wendell Phillips

A simple list such as the following may be all that is necessary for a thirty-minute talk on this subject:

I. Directness

II. Sincerity

III. Enthusiasm

IV. Simplicity

V. Mannerisms

Keep Afloat

For the average speaker, the making of an outline requires painstaking effort. Because the effects upon him are disciplinary, he usually dodges the task. But, as has been demonstrated, the outline affords the speaker a great many advantages. It is like the blueprint in the construction of a ship. It guides the building of a seaworthy vessel. It locates gunnel and galley and determines where the ballast, boilers, bridge, and lifeboats shall be. Without a plan, the boat will flounder, and so will the speaker without an outline.

Between the Lines

To attain oneness, coherence, and emphasis, the speaker must supply transitions and connectives as he moves from point to point. This verbal cement is not generally shown in the outline. Transitions may be either simple words such as *furthermore, since, notwithstanding, despite, in addition, in view of, after all, as a result of,* and others. Or they may be complete sentences and even paragraphs; for example, in the speech outlined by the keyword method above, the specific purpose would be: This is the *kind of speech delivery that is effective.* The transitions might be stated like this: "The first quality in speech delivery that is effective is directness. . . . In addition to being direct in delivery, the speaker must be sincere. . . . Furthermore, directness and sincerity in the effective delivery of a speech depends upon a quality of enthusiasm," and so on.

In every instance, the speaker must *notify his listeners* that he is concluding one idea and introducing another. By this method, elements of the talk can be joined together in a lucid pattern.

Start Now

After reading this discussion of outlining you may react in the fashion described in an old poem:

> The lesson was ended,
> The scholars descended;
> The eels went on eeling;
> The thieves went on stealing;
> Much delighted were they,
> But preferred the old way!

Be different. Make an outline!

CHAPTER XI

STRING YOUR BEADS TO FIT THE LISTENER

"So Sorry"

A JAPANESE STUDENT in a speech class at Northwestern University in the middle thirties was an unusual fellow — personable and brilliant. One of his talks told how to make ideas stick together. He had recently written to his brother in far-off Japan. For the fun of it, he had recorded his mes-sage on a jigsaw post card, disassembled it, put it in an envelope, and mailed it.

In answer, he received a letter of regret from his brother across the sea. It said: "My dear Brother, I have just received your beautiful and most honored post card. But something terrible has happened. It fell out of the envelope in many pieces, and I cannot make it speak to me. So sorry!"

Not a Jigsaw Puzzle

"That," said the student, "is the way it is with too many talks. All the pieces or ideas may be there, but they are so scrambled that no listener can put them together; they make little sense. And because of that everybody is *so sorry.*"

Then he changed the comparison from the jigsaw picture card to talk about beads. "Loose and unorganized ideas are like unstrung beads," he emphasized. No matter where you put them, they are sure to get lost. And unstrung, they are disorganized or unrelated. They are of little use. He pictured his ideas this way: *"Put your thoughts and examples on the string of good organization and hang them around your listeners' mental neck."*

Your speech purposes may be defined and well-phrased yet leave your listeners confused. When this happens, the chances are you have not arranged your ideas into a meaningful, orderly sequence.

A Regiment, Not a Mob

Miscellaneous ideas and information are like members of a mob. Unorganized, they run in all directions, accomplishing no good purpose. But marshaled as a regiment, they achieve the striking power needed to gain their objective.

The problem of organization is something like bringing apples up from the cellar. You have nothing to put them in, and the dozen you try to carry roll hither, thither, and yon. Trying to retrieve some, you lose the others. Now, your objective is clear. You want to convey apples. What you need is a method — a container to hold them together. Some speakers want to get the job of presenting their ideas done without planning, and the result is confusion. Such speakers chase apples of thought all over the place.

The Choice Is Yours

The jigsaw post card, the unstrung beads, the mob, and the spilled apples were all ineffective for want of organization. Speeches also may fail for the same reason. The elements may be there but without intelligible design.

The speaker needs a plan. Such a plan may employ emphasis or climax, cause to effect or effect to cause, simple to complex ideas, familiar to unfamiliar ideas, association of ideas, or special interests.

The plan may be based on chronological or time order. The materials may be arranged according to place relationship or space order. Here, instead of beginning the development of his ideas at a point in time, the speaker treats what he has to say about objects and places according to their position in space, such as front to back or top to bottom. The plan should be selected to fit the audience, the occasion, the material, the speech purpose, and the time allowed the speaker.

Actually, there is no single plan of organization that is best adapted to all needs. The rest of this chapter presents several useful methods of organizing your ideas to fit the listeners.

The Topical Order

The topical or psychological order is one of the most useful methods of speech arrangement. This order is called *psychological* because it enables the speaker to fit his subject to audience interest. By this method he can put his material in the order of strongest, strong, stronger, and thus begin and close his talk impressively.

It is *topical* because the speaker breaks his subject into topics or points of view. He selects only a few points for full treatment rather than many points, each to be touched upon sketchily. His attitude is like that of the old Scandinavian preacher who opened his sermon with these words: "Brudern and Sistern, I komm here tonight to go into great detail upon a few of dose matters dat de Lord has only teched upon lightly."

The main ideas of Van Dyke's talk on his countrymen follows the topical or psychological order. Of the scores of virtues that he might have selected to portray the "Typical Dutchman," he said: "Grant me but six strokes for the picture."*

Assume that you are to speak about Lincoln. You could treat your subject chronologically by talking about him as a boy, as a young lawyer, and as president, or you could use a space order by discussing his life in Washington, Indiana, and Illinois.

In nearly every case, your audience will gain understanding and enjoyment if you limit the geographical area to be discussed or the period of time to be covered; if you treat only one phase of a broad subject or speak only about a sub-class or two of creatures or things.

In your talk on Lincoln, develop psychologically several appealing phases of his life. These could be his speaking power, attitude toward slavery, or insight into the meaning of the Union. You could discuss his honesty, humor, or homeyness, or do as Stewart W. McClelland did in a thirty-minute talk in which he concentrated upon one idea, "Lincoln, the Tolerant":

"This modern prophet brought no new message, just the old one nearly 1900 years old, 'A new commandment write I unto thee, that ye love one another.' The message was not new but the prophet was. Here was one who practiced what he preached, and . . . conquered all his enemies and made them his friends. How can you hate such a man? He licked Jack Armstrong, and Armstrong spent the rest of his life, if we can trust tradition, fighting his battles for him. He vanquished the Little Giant, and Douglas, who wanted the Presidency of the United States more than any other man who ever ran for that office, stood humbly by, holding the hat of his successful rival while the tall,

* See page 116.

gaunt man spoke those beautiful words of the good neighbor, 'We are not enemies, but friends — Though passion may have strained, it must not break our bonds of affection. The mystic chords of memory stretching from every battlefield and patriot grave to every living heart and hearthstone all over this broad land will yet swell the chorus of the Union when again touched, as surely they will be, by the better angels of our nature.' "*

Join the Story Parade

Most audiences love a story. People hunger to become part of a drama. Jesus knew this and taught in parables; for example, read the parable of the Great Supper. By the time the story is told, the speech is made. Its purpose is clearly achieved. The excuse maker is condemned. Less worthy people will receive the rewards he might have had. Jesus announced his point at once: "Blessed is he that shall eat bread in the kingdom of God." The last statement summarizes the basic idea: "For I say unto you, that none of those men which were bidden shall taste of my supper."

An excellent example of the story method is demonstrated in a talk entitled, "Don't Die on Third!" The message is expertly woven into the story. As you read it, note how suspense and drama are deftly combined to maintain interest. The first paragraph provides the setting for the narrative and becomes the *introduction*. The closing paragraph is the *conclusion*. The narrative itself is the *discussion*.

"Don't Die on Third"

It was twenty-five years ago, when the Detroit Tigers were playing the team from Cleveland. The score was a

---

* *Vital Speeches*, Volume VII, Number 12.

tie. It was the last half of the ninth, and two men were out. The fate of the game rested with Moriarty, the white-bloused figure that shuttled back and forth at third base. As the decisive moment approached, Tigers and Naps stood up at their benches, and eighteen thousand spectators bent forward in tense expectancy. Moriarty was on third.

He had come there in the ordinary way. At bat he had hit the ball and run to first. The next batter had bunted and sacrificed to move Moriarty on to second. Then a "long fly" had advanced him to third. There he stood, alert in every nerve, his powerful running legs, his quick eye, and quicker brain holding the hazard of the game.

Much as it means to advance that far, third base runs are not marked up on the scoreboard. Third base is not a destination — it is the last station on the road "home." The world is full of third bases. To leave school, to earn your college degree, to enter a profession is only to start toward third base. To get the job you want, even to become the head of your business, is merely to reach third base.

Third base is opportunity, and opportunity is not arrival; it is only another point of departure. Attain the White House itself, and you have only reached as far as third base. The test of all you have is yet to come. No time for self-applause at third — many a promising run has died there! And there stood Moriarty. If he failed, it was not his failure alone; the team failed with him. Concentrated on him at that moment were the hopes and fears of thousands who seemed to hold their breath. So still was the great park that even the breeze seemed forgetful to blow.

One way to get off third is to wait for someone to bat you off. Another is to get away on your own initiative — Moriarty chose *that*. He knew his game. He knew the catcher's signals called for a ball thrown high to Mullin, who was now at bat. He knew that a runner might duck low to touch the home plate while the catcher's mitt was in the air for a high ball. He knew that in throwing high, pitchers "wind up" in a certain way. He knew also that pitchers have a way of "winding up" when they don't intend to throw. He knew, moreover, that *this* pitcher, being left-handed, could not keep watch on third while delivering the ball and that the runner might safely take a longer lead. *Moriarty knew all the ins and outs of his job.* Luck might lie in the lap of the gods, but *preparation, knowledge, judgment,* and *initiative* were with the player.

Had Moriarty waited for Mullin to bat, Mullin might have failed him, ending the inning. One opening remained: make "home" between the moment the pitch was begun past all recall, and the moment the ball struck the catcher's mitt — make "home" in the fraction of time Mullin's hit or miss hung in futurity. That would be a contest in speed between a five-ounce ball delivered with the force of a superb pitching arm and the hundred-seventy-pound body of Moriarty! An unequal contest, for the pitched ball travels only sixty feet while the runner from third must hurl his body over a distance of ninety feet!

Moriarty is on third. He builds his prospective run as an engineer builds a bridge across a torrent, with infinite pains. Now the Cleveland pitcher is poising himself for a throw. Moriarty is crouched like a tiger ready to spring — *NOW!* There is a white streak across the field! A cloud of dust at the home plate! The umpire stands over it with hands extended, with palms down. The old baseball park echoes and re-echoes with a thunderous roar of acclaim, which bursts forth again and again in thrilling electric power. Every eye strains toward the man who is slapping the dust from his white uniform. *Moriarty is "home!"*

It was only a run made in the course of a baseball game; but it has been saying to us these many years — *Don't die on third.* You may be put out, but it need not be by your inaction. If the run must die, let it die *trying*. All of us are on bases. Some of us are waiting for someone to bat us farther. Suppose he misses! Mullin missed the ball that day — had Moriarty waited, he would not have scored.

It would not be right to say that all the world is a baseball diamond; it *does* offer us the ever-present choice between indolence and initiative; but life's rules are fairer. In life there is an inner scoreboard where every effort is credited to your record. Many a valiant run is lost, but the valor of it builds the soul. So while there's one thing yet to do, and there's always one thing yet to do, or a fraction of time to do it in, *don't die on third.* Study conditions, learn all you can, use all you learn, summon your strength and courage, defy luck — and then, bold player, just by doing this, you have already scored. Something great is strengthened within you. The run may fail, but *you* have not, and there's another game tomorrow.*

Six Honest Serving Men

Rudyard Kipling suggests a method of developing an idea in the following lines:

> I keep six honest serving men
> (They taught me all I knew);
> Their names are What and Why and When
> And How and Where and Who.

When preparing certain kinds of informative talks, you might ask yourself, for example: "What are the four freedoms?" "What do they mean?" "How were they formulated?" "Who formulated them?" "Why?" "When?" "Where?" Such questions will guide your mental digging. They could form the plan of your speech.

Ho Hum !

Here is a simple formula for the effective preparation of a short talk. It is original with Richard Borden and is explained in his fascinating little book, *Public Speaking — As Listeners Like It!* There are four steps in the organization.

1. Ho Hum! (Light a flame of audience interest.)
   This is the introduction.

---

* From a talk given on the Ford Sunday Evening Hour by W. J. Cameron, May 2, 1937.

2. Why bring that up? (Why is interest aroused?) This is the transition from introduction to discussion. It builds a bridge from the island of the listener's interest to the mainland of the speaker's subject.

3. For instance! (Prove the point with examples; get down to cases.) This is the body or discussion.

4. So what? (Restate the point; ask for action.) This is the conclusion. Remember the Chinese proverb: "To talk much and arrive nowhere is the same as climbing a tree to catch a fish."*

Emerson Is Right

Here is a student talk in which this formula is used:

Ho hum! Nearly a million Americans will go to jail this year for breaking the law. No doubt each of them believed he would never be found out.

Why bring that up? While none of us here may ever go to jail, too many of us are guilty of conduct that is not right and honest. We leave our cars in "no parking" zones; we ignore speed limits, stop signs, and traffic regulations. Besides fouling the traffic lanes, we risk cheating in examinations and sometimes lie about age and qualifications to filch a little personal gain. We sow the seeds of moral debt, and the harvest can be bitter.

For instance! My recent experience overwhelmingly demonstrates that even the most obscure of our actions may arise to embarrass us in unexpected ways.

I live in Eastern Utah. My folks are in the cattle business. This last summer, I helped my father on the range

---

* Richard C. Borden, *Public Speaking — As Listeners Like It!* pp. 3-12. Harper and Brothers, New York. 1935. Reprinted by permission.

with the stock. While returning to camp about sundown one day, I spied a plump, two-point buck. At this season it was unlawful to kill a deer. But I was hungry for venison, and, reasoning that I was so far away from anybody that I would never be detected, I raised my gun and shot him. I prepared the carcass and took the choice parts to camp. My father was most displeased about my transgression of the law. But he agreed that since the buck was dead, we had better not waste the meat. So we cooked and ate a venison supper.

The next day as I worked among the cattle, I became violently ill. I grew rapidly worse and was driven hurriedly to a doctor, who performed an emergency operation for the removal of my appendix.

As I revived after surgery, the doctor greeted me with a grave and troubled look. He said he was chagrined to discover that he had just saved the life of a lawbreaker. He didn't think he'd turn me over to the sheriff, but he was certain that he should. In response to my puzzled and uneasy questioning, the doctor announced that I had just eaten freshly killed deer meat. He declared that the evidence was indisputable. Thereupon, he stretched before my bulging eyes, a long, coarse, gray hair that was newly lost from the hide of the deer. The hair was the reason for my trouble. While I was eating the meat, it had lodged in my appendix, causing acute inflammation.

So what? I learned an important lesson from this unhappy experience. I learned that Emerson is right in his essay on "Compensation": "Persons and events may stand for a time between you and justice, but it is only a postponement. You must pay at last your own debt . . . . You cannot do wrong without suffering wrong." My transgression had found me out and taught me that all wrongdoers finally face at least the penalty of humiliation.

Carnegie's Variation on a Theme by Borden

Dale Carnegie uses a variation of this organization in his widely-acclaimed course in public speaking and human relations. He calls it the *Magic Formula*:

1. Ho hum !
2. Point.
3. Reason.
4. For example.
5. So what ?

Carnegie divides the "Why bring that up?" of the Borden formula into a statement of *point* and *reason* to follow the lighting of the fire of audience interest in the "Ho hum!"

An "Impromptu" by Collins

You may have knowledge and background on a subject and be called to talk unexpectedly. To avoid making your speech a jumble of ideas, use either the "Ho hum" plans or this one by Collins, which is especially adapted to the spur-of-the-moment talk.

Mentally ask yourself three questions in the preparation step:

1. What will I ask the audience to do about the subject?
2. What general truth concerning the subject can I present ?
3. What actual experience can I think of that will illustrate the general truth ?

When you *deliver* the talk, *reverse the procedure:*

1. Relate and describe the illustration from human experience.
2. Emphasize the general truth as suggested by your illustration.
3. Tie the illustration and the general truth together in an impressive statement and request action.*

Proof Follows Point

There are two common methods of establishing the proof for a statement as outlined in *Principles and Types of Speech* by Professor Alan Monroe. The first of these he calls the *didactic method,* and says: "This is perhaps the clearest and most obvious method of assembling your proof; it can be outlined as follows:

1. State your point.
2. Make it clear by explanation, comparison, or illustration.
3. Support it by additional factual illustrations, specific instances, statistics, or testimony.
4. Restate your point as the conclusion."

If you have several reasons or points in the development of your purpose, you can add units of this organiza-

---

* George R. Collins, *Platform Speaking,* p. 177. Harper and Brothers, New York. 1923. Reprinted by permission.

tional device, connecting one to the other with sentences or paragraphs of transition.

Point Follows Proof

Professor Monroe explains that the second method consists of presenting the facts first, from which the conclusion inevitably must be drawn. It is called the *method of implication*. The conclusion is stated at the end, after the evidence to support it has been presented.

It is more truly the method "by which we reach conclusions ourselves, uninfluenced by another person" and is "more persuasive with the listeners. It avoids making them feel that you are pushing something down their throats. It is, in fact, almost the only method to use with an audience that is hostile to the point you wish to present." An outline of this method follows:

"1. Present an analogy or illustration which *implies* the point you wish to make.
2. Present additional illustrations, instances, figures, and testimony which point inevitably to the conclusion without stating it.
3. Show how these facts lead unavoidably to this conclusion; use explanation, if necessary.

4. Definitely state your point as a conclusion."

Of the elements that make up these techniques, Professor Monroe points out: "Explanation, comparison, and illustration are primarily useful in making an idea clear and vivid, while instances, statistics, and testimony have the function of establishing and verifying its truth and importance. Restatement, of course, serves to emphasize and to assist the memory."*

Suppose you were to talk to an audience, for example, that favored socialized medicine. Assume your purpose is to oppose it. You select the method of *point follows proof*. You begin your talk without announcing the point you wish to make. Instead, you present an illustration that brings out the disappointing record of socialized medicine in England. You might follow this by relating its failures in New Zealand and elsewhere. You would then submit statistics from these countries to reinforce your illustrations. You would quote the testimony of experts to give emphasis to the idea that socialized medicine is an inefficient system. You might use a factual or figurative analogy or comparison to heighten the audience feeling about the futility of such a program. You would show how all of these facts and materials lead to one inevitable conclusion. Finally, you would definitely state your point in such a way as to force the choice of "this or nothing."

The Point

The following excerpt shows how Aaron M. Sargent, member of the San Francisco Bar, states his point in the conclusion of his talk on "Socialized Medicine":

---

* Alan H. Monroe, *Principles and Types of Speech*, pp. 241-42. Scott, Foresman and Company, Chicago. 1949. Reprinted by permission.

"You had better think about the effect of all this on the morale of our people. Every time we lead men to believe they can get something for nothing, we bring them closer to dictatorship. Lenin said 'socialized medicine is the keystone to the arch of the socialist state.'

"There are at least ten communist fronts working for social insurance. Do you think they are trying to improve conditions in the United States? Do you have the idea they are trying to build a strong nation able to stand up against Soviet Russia ?

"No, the key people in these communist fronts realize that compulsory health insurance will bankrupt the United States, as it has exhausted the finances of every nation which has tried that experiment. They know disorder will follow — that we will become disunited. And they know something else — they realize that controls established under that system will be available to set up a dictatorship.

"*Social Security is the greatest delusion of our time.* We have come to believe we can get security without working for it — that it is only necessary to vote for it. The people of another great nation went to destruction because of their belief in that delusion. They voted for a promise of their leader. He said: '*We shall banish want. We shall banish fear. The essence of National Socialism is human welfare. National Socialism is the revolution of the common man. National Socialism means a new day of abundance at home, and a better world abroad.*' Those are the words of *Adolf Hitler,* and that is the delusion.

"What does America intend to do about its own delusion? What do you propose to do about it?"*

---

* *Vital Speeches,* Volume XV, Number 10.

CHAPTER XII

LADIES AND GENTLEMEN: THE SPEAKER

FEW OF US escape the responsibility of introducing a speaker. During World War II, the writer was invited to present an explorer whose subject was "Alaska." During the interview the lecturer related this experience: "On the campus of a university where I was scheduled to speak, I met a long-lost friend who pumped my hand and exclaimed, 'I'm just the one to introduce you. I knew you in Alaska. I'll create atmosphere for your talk.' That he did — by reciting 'The Spell of the Yukon,' 'The Shooting of Dan McGrew,' and 'The Cremation of Sam McGee.' "

Oh, yes, that reminds me, there's just one more, "The Spell of the Yukon," and *then* our main speaker.

After forty-five minutes of *creating atmosphere,* he finally remembered the speaker of the evening. Too many introductions are like this. They display the talents of the wrong person.

Winning Friends for the Speaker

The purpose of an introduction is to bring the speaker and his audience together, creating a friendly eagerness on the part of the listeners, arousing curiosity about him and his subject, making the audience respect and like him.

OBSERVE THESE RULES:

1. Speak briefly. Do not exceed two or three minutes. Cut your remarks in half if you can.

2. Avoid stale and stilted phrases such as: "We are indeed honored . . . It is a rare privilege . . . It is my delightful pleasure . . . We are met here to-night, etc. . . ."

3. Do not embarrass the speaker by predicting the in-describable treat that the audience is about to enjoy or by a flowery statement of the speaker's achieve-ments and qualifications. Even a wonderful speaker cannot surmount the high wall of irrational audi-ence expectation. Understatement is better than overstatement. Let the speaker surprise the audience with the degree of his excellence.

4. Do not steal the limelight from the speaker by taking his time, by previewing the contents of his talk, by demonstrating what a superior speaker you are, by entertaining the audience at the expense of the speaker, or by showing off in general.

5. Do not introduce a speaker you do not know. If he is not known to you personally, do some research and arrange an interview with him for a few un-hurried moments. Check the contents of your in-troduction with the speaker.

6. Remember, the greater the man the shorter the introduction.

7. Don't give your speaker false starts by announcing his name and then going on with additional com-

ments. If he bobs up and down because of your misleading entrance cues, you can easily upset his timing and composure.

8. After you have stated the speaker's subject, announce his name clearly, bow slightly as he comes forward, and when he recognizes you, sit down.

9. Leave the platform if you can. But if you remain on the stand during the speech, do not whisper with anyone or go to sleep. Set a good example by your own attentive listening.

10. When the speaker finishes, don't rehash the speech to drive his point home. Thank him graciously and adjourn.

Answer These Questions

These are the essential questions an audience wants answered when the speaker is introduced: "*Why this subject? Why this subject for us? Why this subject for us at this time? Why this subject for us at this time by this speaker?*"*

This guide is basically sound but must be adapted to the occasion; for example, in the following introduction you will observe that the emphasis is placed upon the speaker. The importance of the subject is not given more stress here only because it had been previously established with the audience. In this instance, the pertinent question being answered is, "Why this speaker before this audience on this subject?"

---

*Adapted from Richard C. Borden, *Public Speaking — As Listeners Like It* p. 36. Harper and Brothers, New York. 1935.

You're On . . .

Picture Mr. Guy Toombs, jovial manager of the Hotel Utah, arising to present the luncheon speaker to his fellow Rotarians.

"Fellows: Columbus discovered America; Sutter discovered gold; Madame Curie discovered radium; but my great discovery years ago was Ep Hoyt. So stimulating and challenging for me was this discovery that I secured the help of Rotarian Johnny Fitzpatrick of the Salt Lake *Tribune*, to persuade Ep Hoyt to address our club today. He will speak on the most important subject of our time — World Peace!

"John and I matched dollars to see who would introduce Ep. He lost, and since he's on the Board of Directors of the hotel, I'm a little shaky about my future around here. But the honor of introducing my distinguished friend is so great, I'm going to take a chance.

"By training and experience, S. Palmer Hoyt is eminently fitted to discuss the problem of peace. He enlisted as a private in World War I and advanced to the rank of sergeant-major with the A. E. F. He has been reporter, city editor, executive news editor, and finally managing editor and publisher of the great Portland *Oregonian*.

"In May 1943, when he joined Elmer Davis in the work of the Office of War Information, Mr. Davis lauded his integrity and talents.

"And as Ep took up his duties with the Denver *Post* about a year ago, Governor Dewey praised him 'as one of the great editors of our time.'

"In view of his vast experience as soldier and editor, and because of his ability to think and speak on world problems, he is *the* man to talk on the subject — *Our Last Good Hope For Peace.* Fellow Rotarians, I am going to announce him as did the headlines proclaiming his arrival in Denver to become editor of the *Post* — '*Hell's Bells, It's Hoyt!*' "

This introduction is informal, yet tells the audience what it wants to know. It contains some good-natured "kidding," which is enjoyed by members of the Rotary Club. When you introduce speakers, use a little humor if it fits. Nothing is better than a bit of congenial laughter to create a friendly feeling.

If you cannot apply the principles which successfully launch the speaker, you might emulate the chairman who said, "I have been asked to introduce Senator Reed who will speak to you. Now I have done it. Now he will do it!"

CHAPTER XIII

MODERN KNIGHTS OF THE ROUND TABLE

SHAKESPEARE SAID, "An old man is twice a child." John D. Rockefeller became one of the richest men in America. He lived to be ninety-eight years old, but due to the frailty of his health he lived on human milk for nearly half his life. How will you and I end our days? In the springtime of youth budding hope promises romance and adventure, but in the autumn and winter of life what prospect is there for happiness?

Finding an answer to this question and others like it is best accomplished by group thinking. There are several ways in which people participate in discussion: the panel, forum, symposium, debate, and conference. In each of these the skill with which the individual thinks and expresses himself determines the success of the deliberations.

Around the Round Table

Picture Robert J. Havighurst, professor of education, and Dr. John A. Schindler, practicing physician, rubbing mental elbows "around the Round Table" at the University of Chicago. They are seeking an answer to the question "How to Live A Hundred Years Happily!"*

A study of the transcript of their discussion will enable you to discover important techniques of communication. As you read, be alert for the answers to these questions:

1. Are the learned men making a display of their erudition? Or is their language and expression

---

*Robert J. Havighurst and John A. Schindler, "How to Live a Hundred Years Happily!" in *The University of Chicago Round Table*, Number 607. Chicago, Nov. 6, 1949. Reprinted by permission. The marginal notes and the insertion of discussion steps are the writer's.

simple and direct like conversation? Does it have the "homey touch"?

2. Do the speakers clarify their points through well-chosen illustration? Or do they generalize and reason in the abstract?

3. Are there any light touches of humor in the discussion? Is the problem freighted with professorial jargon and dignity?

4. How are questions used to advance the work of the panel? Are they a vital aid to cooperation? Do they illuminate obscure points and encourage participation or are they merely clever traps to trick the speakers?

5. Is the general tone of the proceedings one of friendly inquiry, genuine cooperation, and open-mindedness or one of sharp disagreement and dogmatic opinion?

6. Does the discussion lead to possible solutions? Does it leave the audience confused and uncertain?

How to Live a Hundred Years Happily!

(What is the trouble?)

MR. HAVIGHURST: We see more people eighty years old and over than ever before. We know that **Facts** there are more people a hundred years old than ever before. We know that more of us middle-aged people than we realize are going to live to be a hundred. Medical science is adding more years to our lives.

DR. SCHINDLER: The facts which you have just cited introduce another important consideration. After **Explanation** all, there is no use getting to be seventy or eighty or a hundred or even fifty, for that mat-

ter, if you cannot be reasonably happy doing it. And, by
and large, most people taken at any age do not seem to me

Testimony   to be happy, at least those I meet as a physician
are either sick because they are unhappy or
they are unhappy because they are sick. And
my observation is that unhappiness tends to

Question   increase with age. What is your opinion?

(What are the causes of the trouble?)

MR. HAVIGHURST: Yes, I think so, too. At the University
of Chicago we have been studying older people,

Authority   trying to find out what makes some of them
happy and some of them unhappy. You might

say that we have asked older people to write us a prescription for happiness in the later years. We find four things
to be most productive of happiness. They are, first, health,

good health; and, second, a comfortable place

Facts   to live and enough money to live on (though
one man's plenty is another man's poverty, and

there is no definite amount of money which will meet the
needs of all kinds of people); third, recognition and approval by one's neighbors and family and community (we
tend to approve ourselves when other people approve us);
and fourth, social participation — that is, taking part with
other people in social and business and community activities. Unhappy old age really commences, I think, when a

person is cut off from other persons.

Question   What do you think of this prescription for
a happy old age, Doctor?

Appreciation DR. SCHINDLER: You have given an excellent
four-point view of happiness.

As a physician, of course, my chief concern is the
health of these elderly people. . . . It seems to me that to

**Limiting
Problem**

arrive at an understanding of what makes happiness in old age we have to talk about the things that make for unhappiness, and maybe in the course of that gabfest we can define happiness and get some idea as to what it is.

Statistics

Definition

Now, the first amazing and astonishing medical fact today is that between thirty-five and fifty percent of all the people who are sick are sick principally because they are unhappy; that unhappiness produces a disease which we call a psychosomatic illness. It excepts no one. Anybody in any walk of life can get this disease. But the fact is that the number of people with psychosomatic illness actually increases with age simply because the cares and difficulties which produce unhappiness increase with age. . . .

**Factual
Illustration**

The case history of the stage manager in the theater, I think, is typical. He was an elderly man of eighty-two, jumping around the stage as spry as a little cricket. In his earlier days he had been the stage manager of a theater on Broadway. When he got too old, he lost his job and drifted to second-rate theaters, then to third-rate, and, finally, into the care of some of his relatives in San Francisco, where he had little affection and gradually became more and more debilitated. There in bed a fine young physician found him; took him to the Municipal Home; and when he got him there, he said, "We're building a theater here, and we need a stage manager. We'd sure like to have a stage manager from Broadway."

And the little old man said, "I'm your stage manager."

Within a short time he was remarkably active, and the only evidence of degenerative disease which he had when I saw him was hardening of the arteries, which certainly did not hold him down very much.

MR. HAVIGHURST: You say, Doctor, that this man's unhappiness and inactivity are what made him **Questions** sick and not his arteries? Is this just a figure of speech to say that unhappiness is the cause of disease? How can a disease be caused by unhappiness? And is it right to call it a real disease?

DR. SCHINDLER: The cause for a psychosomatic illness certainly boils down to just one thing — unhappiness. And believe me, Havighurst, it is a terrifically real **Restatement** disease. It is not a disease in which the patient just thinks that he is sick. It can mimic any other disease which you wish to name. It can produce pain and malfunction in any organ. And it is a disease which is brought on by the constant repetition of unpleasant emotions, such as anxiety, fear, apprehension, discouragement, and disappointment . . . .

Now, the importance of not only apprehension but also the constant monotonous repetition of apprehension in bringing about a psychosomatic illness was **Authority** shown beautifully by Little and Hart, of Cornell, in an experiment which they made upon sheep. On the leg of one sheep in a field out in the state of New York they tied a light wire. This sheep could carry this wire around without any difficulty; and they gave small electric shocks over the wire. All that this **Factual** small shock produced was a slight twitching **Illustration** of the leg in the sheep. The sheep went on perfectly normally. But Dr. Little and Dr. Hart were able to produce a psychosomatic illness in that sheep by simply producing apprehension and regularity in the shocks. This they did by warning the sheep ten seconds ahead of time, by ringing a bell, that it was going to be shocked. But they had to repeat this apprehensive shock monotonously in order really to affect the sheep. Very soon the sheep ceased eating. It did not associate with its fellow sheep any more; it was a totally different animal.

Comparison

Questions

MR. HAVIGHURST: Just how do unpleasant emotions produce physical illness? You have indicated that in the case of the sheep — and I presume similarly in the case of human beings — that the repetition of these unpleasant emotions makes the individual become ill. But can you describe in language which the layman can understand? What is the bodily process?

Definition

by

Authority

Repetition

DR. SCHINDLER: The easiest path to the understanding of the psychosomatic illness is through the definition of emotions given us by William James, as far back as 1888 — a definition which has not been improved upon. James said that an emotion is a state of mind (mark that, a state of mind) manifesting itself — that is showing itself — by a sensible change in the body. Let me repeat that: An emotion is a state of mind manifesting itself by a sensible change in the body.

Let us take a concrete emotion — anger — a very common one. There is a state of mind, of course, which calls for the emotion of anger, and the manifestations which

occur in the body are of two kinds. One kind is the type
you can see. The face gets red; the eyes widen;
Description the fists clench; the muscles tremble; the voice
has a tremor — those are the external manifestations. But there are internal manifestations which are
often more acute and more terrific than the external ones;
for instance, in anger the blood immediately coagulates
quicker; the red count of the blood immediately goes up;
and the muscles at the outlet of the stomach will squeeze
down so hard that the stomach will not empty during the
state of anger. Also, the muscles of the small intestine and
the colon will often squeeze down so hard that after the
emotion of anger is over, the individual will have an acute
stomach ache. The repetition of any emotion
Restatement which produces muscle spasm, will eventually
result in pain, just as though you clenched
your fist real hard. . . .

Now, if this spasm involves the blood vessels on the
heart, then, of course, you have a very serious
Factual condition. John Hunter, one of the greatest
Illustration physiologists England ever had, had that kind
of heart. Every time he became angry, the blood vessels
on his heart would squeeze down so hard that he would
have a terrific pain, which we call angina pec-
Definition toris, and he always said that if anybody ever
got him real angry, that person would kill him.
And that is exactly what happened. At a medical meeting
he got up to dispute something with which he disagreed,
and became so angry that he dropped dead.

Now, most of the headaches which we have,
Explanation and half of all the ulcer-like pain, half of all
the gall-bladder-like pain, ninety-nine and

Statistics   forty-four one-hundredths percent of what we call gas or bloating, much of our constipation and diarrhea are produced by this emotional mechanism, as well as, also, urinary frequency very often, and about thirty percent of the muscular rheumatism, and even thirty percent of our skin rashes.

MR. HAVIGHURST: All right. A great deal of the illness, especially of older people, is produced by un-
Restatement pleasant emotions, and these emotions actually cause damage in the body. But how can we
Questions use this knowledge about which we have been talking? How can we cure this kind of illness?

DR. SCHINDLER: The cure of psychosomatic illness is actually very simple. One has only to substitute for the unpleasant emotions such as anxiety, fear, appre-
Explanation hension, disappointment, the pleasant emo-
tions such as confidence, assurance, pleasant expectancy, joy, and hope, because these pleasant emotions produce the optimal tone of the muscles and the optimal function of the endocrine glands which we feel when we say to ourselves, "Gee, I'm feeling good!"

MR. HAVIGHURST: . . . . With these kinds of real cares and difficulties and troubles, how do you go about
Question curing the illness which is brought about by them ?

(What are the possible solutions?)

DR. SCHINDLER: . . . . It would be perfectly idiotic to tell these people, or anybody else, that they can keep their atti-tude cheerful and pleasant all the time, but the idea is to keep it pleasant and cheerful as much of the time as pos-sible. Some of the general advice in facilitating the effectiveness in this key thought is this: First of all, we tell these people that they should not be constantly on the lookout for signs of ill health. Look for illness, and it will be sure to come via the psychosomatic route. In the second place, keep usefully at work, if you are old, even in a chair. One of the quickest ways to illness, and even to death, is to retire too hard. And, third, have a hobby — something which turns at least part of your existence into pleasure and pleasurable expectancy. An elderly patient of mine **Specific** had alienated her entire family by constantly **Illustration** telling them how miserable she felt.

The fourth point is: Learn to be satisfied. I mean by that, of course, to be satisfied when the situation is such that you cannot easily change it or when you are in a situation in which dissatisfaction is not going to be of some use. Learn to be satisfied. It is just as easy, . . . and it is much more pleasurable.

And, fifth, keep on liking people. You have to live with them. Their ways and views may not be yours, but that is probably because of difference in your age. . . .

And, sixth, meet adversity valiantly. Age is often beset by adversity; and, when it comes, get up and try to go on. We had a man who was in bed a year. **Factual** Three months before he got sick, his wife had **Illustration** died. A month later his son was killed. And from then on, all he could think of was, "Why did this have to happen to me? . . . He carried on in that vein until he became very sick. He had not learned to accept adversity. A lot of people start psychosomatic illness after adversity.

Then, the seventh thing is to meet your little problems of everyday life with decision. Do not keep mulling them over in your mind. It is that which brings on a psychosomatic illness. If you have a problem, decide what you are going to do about it, and then quit thinking about it.

And, the eighth thing is, above all, maintain a good sense of humor; and this is best done by getting in the habit of saying something pleasant every time you get a chance.

Humorous Illustration I had a patient by the name of Sam who had never, so far as anybody knew, said anything humorous or pleasant in his life. . . . Sam's mind worked like this: One early day in July I went past his farm and saw a beautiful field of oats on his farm, and I thought, "Well, this should make Sam happy." I stopped in at the barnyard, saw Sam, and said, "Sam, that's a wonderful field of oats."

And he countered by saying, "Yeah, but the wind'll blow it down before I get it cut." He was worried about

that. I watched his field that week and saw that he got it cut all right. He had it threshed. I knew he got a good price for it — that was two years ago. So I thought, "Well, now I've got Sam where he has to say something pleasant."

The next time that I saw him I said, "Sam, how did that field of oats turn out?"

And he said, "Well, I guess the crop was all right, and I guess the price was about as good as you can expect, but you know, a field of oats like that sure takes a lot out of the soil."

And two months later . . . . I said, "Sam, this is a wonderful day, isn't it?" I said it real enthusiastically, to try to make it contagious.

And Sam said, "Yeah, but when we get it, we'll get it hard."

Restatement People like Sam invariably get a psychosomatic illness. . . . They are cares to their families, and there is nothing you can do for them.

And the ninth, and last point, is live to make the present hour pleasant and cheerful. Keep your mind out of the past and keep it out of the future.

(What is the best solution?)

These nine points, I think, facilitate a great deal of use of the key thought, which is: I will keep my attitude and thinking cheerful and as pleasant as possible.

MR. HAVIGHURST: . . . I suggest that we close this discussion with another look at happiness. Have we come any closer to an understanding of this thing called "happiness"?

DR. SCHINDLER: Do you think that possibly in talking about unhappiness we have really been defining happiness? Is happiness not the state of mind in which our thinking is pleasant a good share of the time? If any of you radio listeners have any better definition of happiness, I wish that you would send it either to Havighurst or myself; and that is it — that is how to live to be a hundred happily.

The Job of the Panel

Thinking begins with a problem or felt difficulty. To find an answer or solution is the purpose of the panel. Every individual could profit from the experience of deliberating with others to find the answers to questions of mutual concern. Talking them over together is democracy at work and is the best of all the methods of resolving misunderstandings.

After the problem is decided upon, the panel members are selected. Although the foregoing example had only two participants, there may be as many as six or eight. Too many panel members can make progress slow and laborious. If you are one of the panel, gather all the information you possibly can. Arrange interviews with authorities on some aspect of the problem, read widely, make extensive and un-biased investigations. Organize the data and become thor-oughly familiar with your materials.

You should have a preliminary meeting with the other members of the panel. Here you can become acquainted with their points-of-view and exchange data. Your ideas will probably differ from those of the others inasmuch as each of you talked to different people and examined differ-ent sources.

When the panel meets for its discussion, the members pool their knowledge, analyze the data carefully, and talk about the problem from every angle. Since inquiry is the fundamental objective, the members of the panel and audi-ence resent dogmatic assertions but desire information that will enable them to think intelligently and to formulate their own opinions. The discussion is carried on without script.

Etiquette at the Round Table

Panel members are grouped in a semi-circle with the chairman in the center. Members and audience (if there is one) are visible to each other. The chairman will set forth briefly the essential background of the problem and the reason for the discussion. He will present the panel members to each other and the audience in a way that will establish a pleasant and informal atmosphere.

The chairman will insist — gently, but firmly — on fairness. He will restrain the overly aggressive members and encourage the timid. He will guide the discussion so that the main problem is explored and irrelevant materials kept at a minimum. He will budget the time and summarize briefly as the discussion moves from step to step or whenever the main issue is obscured.

He may say, "We are agreed, then, on these points," or "The problem now resolves itself into this." He will close the panel in the time allotted. The duration will depend upon the circumstances. He will conclude the meeting with a final clear, terse statement of the best solution or the opinion of the majority. Cooperation rather than competition is the prevailing spirit.

When to Speak

"1. *When you are asked a question.* This is so obvious that it would not require comment were it not for the fact that one often remains silent when he does not know an answer. In such a case it is better to say frankly, 'I don't know,' than to delay the discussion by attempting to evade the question by silence.

"2. *When you can clarify a vague point made by another.* Often the knowledge you possess or your facility of expression will make it possible to bring to a point a jumbled comment made by another. The other members of the group will thank you for this service.

"3. *When you can correct an error.* This should by all means be done in order that the conclusions of the group may be correct. Be careful, however, not to be officious in making the correction. Be courteous and modest.

"4. *When you can present illustrations, statistics, or testimony which will clarify the point under discussion.* No one knows everything about any subject, but by combining the knowledge of the members of the group, a sounder judgment and understanding may be achieved. One should be sure, however, that the facts he presents have a direct bearing on the point at issue.

"5. *When you can ask an intelligent question.* Although it is unwise to be continually asking questions, it is occasionally necessary to do so. Remember that if you are in doubt about some matter, there are doubtless others in the group in a similar position. Often a subject causes difficulty because it is too big as a whole, but it can be divided into more understandable parts by a properly-timed question."

When asking a question, remember Franklin's words: "Virtue is obtained rather by the use of the ear than of the tongue — put on the humble inquirer."

How to Speak

"1. *Don't be a verbal peacock.* You will be observed by others, and what you say may be discredited. The 'smart aleck' has no place either in the classroom or in commercial circles."

Pay attention to what is being said all the time. The daydreamer will find himself mentally undressed when it is his turn to appear.

"2. *Do not hesitate when you can contribute.* Fear and a false sense of modesty are frequently responsible for people maintaining silence when they might benefit others as well as themselves by venturing an opinion. When the opportunity presents itself, speak up immediately — a minute's delay, and the chance may be gone.

"3. *Talk loud enough to be heard.* This does not mean to be boisterous and 'loudmouthed.' Such conduct is bad, particularly at a social gathering. Most people err in the other direction, however; especially is this true in the classroom where students often mumble devoid of all meaning. To avoid misunderstanding, speak up.

"4. *Speak to the point; do not ramble.* In group discussion, time is valuable. Be brief. A few concise comments properly developed by a pointed illustration or by statistics are more valuable than an extended dissertation. State one idea and stick to it; do not try to say too much at once.

"5. *Be modest in manner, but positive in statement.* The arrogant individual is seldom welcome. On the other hand, those who vacillate in their opinions or make too many qualifications about their comments are not often respected. If you believe a thing, say so definitely but modestly. Let your words say, 'This is so,' but let your personal bearing add, 'If I am wrong, I am willing to be corrected.'

"6. *Accept criticism or correction with dignity.* Most persons, when they offer criticism, do so with kindly intent. When you are corrected or reproved, weigh the justice of criticism, follow the succeeding discussion with even closer attention, and calmly resume your part in it."*

The panel discussion should include the following steps:

1. Define the problem and the terms used. Make certain all the members are agreed on what is to be discussed. Direct remarks to the question: *What is the trouble?*

2. Analyze the problem and its origin. Set up standards by which to evaluate possible solutions. Direct remarks to the question: *What are the causes of the trouble?*

3. Find the possible solutions to the problem. Direct remarks to the question: *What are the possible solutions?*

4. Compare the various solutions of the problem or trouble. Direct remarks to the question: *What merits or defects are inherent in each?*

5. Select and test the solution which appears to be the best. Direct remarks to the question: *What is the best possible solution?*

Symposium

In the symposium several speakers present their own answers to one general question. "America's Town Meeting of the Air" is an excellent example. From two to four recognized experts talk from five to ten minutes apiece.

---

*Alan H. Monroe and Paul E. Lull, *Projects in Speech for a Foundation Course*, p. 143. D. C. Heath and Co., Chicago. 1931. Reprinted by permission.

Each speaker stands before the audience and presents his views from a prepared statement. The chairman acts as moderator. After all the individuals have spoken, a panel of the symposium speakers may be formed for further exploration of the problem. The chairman will conclude the panel with a brief summary. Following the panel discussion, the audience is usually invited to ask questions of the various speakers. The answers generally submit a more detailed explanation or reveal weakness in the argument. Often the speaker who is in agreement with the questioner seizes the opportunity to elaborate upon a point of view already expressed. The purpose of the combination symposium-panel is to arouse awareness in the listener of the validity of opposite positions.

Conference

Borden and Busse in their volume *The New Public Speaking* outline a method of introducing ideas for the consideration of a group in conference. They recommend the following parliamentary procedure: Rise from your seat and call out, "Mr. Chairman!" in a clear, audible voice. Remain standing until the chairman recognizes you as the next speaker. Then follow this procedure:

"1. Explain to your conferees a *need*.

2. Explain the *cause* of that need.

3. Explain what you believe to be the *remedy* for that need.

4. Offer a resolution which states the remedy *in a manner that your group can accept and act upon*.

5. Move the *adoption* of the resolution."*

---

* Richard C. Borden and Alvin C. Busse, *The New Public Speaking*, p. 7 Harper and Brothers, New York. 1930. Reprinted by permission.

A Final Check

The effective speaker will adapt his remarks to the viewpoint of his listeners. He will appeal to their motives and identify his proposition with what they already believe. When organizing his speech, he will measure his preparation against a check list such as the following:

1. Have I made my idea clear ?

2. Have I made it arresting ?

3. Have I made it attractive ?

4. Have I made it familiar ?

5. Have I made it significant ?

6. Have I made it appealing ?

7. Have I made it convincing ?

8. Have I made it inevitable ?*

For coherence the speaker will employ the formula of the Negro preacher:

"Fust Ah tells 'em what ah's gwine tell 'em;
Den, Ah tells 'em;
Den, Ah tells 'em what Ah done tole 'em."

---

* Adapted from Robert T. Oliver, Rupert L. Cortright, and Cyril F. Hager, *The New Training for Effective Speech*, p. 142. The Dryden Press, New York. 1946.

CHAPTER XIV

FROM START TO FINISH

A RAILWAY EMPLOYEE accidentally trapped himself in a refrigerator car. He could neither escape nor attract the attention of anybody to his sad plight, so he resigned himself to a tragic fate. The record of his approaching death was scribbled on the wall of the car in these words: "I am becoming colder. Still colder now. Nothing to do but wait . . . . These may be my last words." And they were.

When the car was opened, the searchers were astonished to find him dead. There was no physical reason for his death. The temperature of the car was a moderate fifty-six degrees. Only in the mind of the victim did the freezing apparatus ever work. There was plenty of fresh air. He hadn't suffocated. He died of his own fears.*

Similar tragedies occur in the thoughts of speakers — not, of course, to the extent of snuffing out actual human life. But the results are dire. Enthusiasm of speaker, appeal of speech, and interest of audience are all effectually killed. When a speaker uses the destructive power of negative suggestion, he plants, perhaps unknowingly, ideas in the minds of both himself and listeners that suggest lack of preparation, boredom, and failure.

Alchemy of Mind

An eminent authority in selling describes the effect of suggestion upon the attitudes of the speaker and his audience:

"The most important factor in the delivery of a talk is not the listener. It is not the subject. It is not the purpose.

---

* A true story told by Dudley Cavert.

It is not even the material. It is not the occasion. It is not the weather, nor the season of the year.

"It is the speaker himself — the person behind the speech — the individual who delivers.

"And the most important factor on the speaker's part in presenting his talk is his attitude. . . .

"As you know, there is a strange alchemy of mind which no one quite understands, yet every scientist recognizes. We know that we transmit our thoughts, our feelings, our expectations, our exultations, our fears, our doubts to those to whom we speak . . . ."*

Avoid the Big I

The unguarded speaker can artlessly convey this "strange alchemy of mind" in a manner that destroys the interest of the audience and may even be revolting, par-

ticularly when he brings himself excessively into the foreground of the speech. At a service-club meeting, this point was brought forcibly home to the writer. The speaker said: "I went to India where I met some nice people. I was treated wonderfully. One man especially was attentive to me. He said he'd take me to dinner if I'd meet him later at the New Delhi Hotel." So what? Is there anything about such personal details that will interest an audience? When personal experiences are used

---

* Charles B. Roth, *Secrets of Closing Sales*, pp. 21-22. Prentice-Hall, Inc., New York. 1947. Reprinted by permission. The author has paraphrased the first three paragraphs and last line to apply to public speaking.

they must not suggest a desire to display one's self. They should be more than mere chitchat.

Another displeasing practice is illustrated in the talk of the person who says, "I went to the Grand Canyon, and what a thrill I got! I tell you, it was tremendous." Such personal reference is important only if it says something that will express an idea of greater importance than the telling. The speaker must draw his listeners into the picture. He might say, "We are about to view one of the world's most astonishing natural wonders. Come with me to the brink of the Grand Canyon. See those sheer walls that drop straight down into the chasm for nearly a mile. Catch a glimpse of the silver ribbon that winds in and out at the bottom of the gorge. That is the roaring Colorado River. And off in the distance, veiling the endless plateaus, is a blue haze hanging like a curtain . . . ."

Subdue Self-Interest

Yield not to the temptation to say: "My thoughts on the subject are . . . . I know I'm right when I say . . . . I achieved a great deal of pleasure . . . . My experiences are truly remarkable . . . ."

Here is a golden rule for speakers: *Subdue your own self-interest.* Instead of "*I*," say "*You.*"

For the introduction, the body, and the conclusion to fulfil their function, use positive suggestion in each. An otherwise excellent speech can be ruined by the negative attitudes of the speaker. It is by his use of suggestion that his skill is really tested. Particularly is this true in the introduction and conclusion where the speaker greets and takes leave of his audience. Here the temptation to digress into a discussion of himself and his shortcomings is most alluring.

A good introduction avoids directing the attention of the audience to the egotism of the speaker as expressed in apology and "phony" self-abasement. An attempt at artificial humility is a common indulgence even with some speakers of acknowledged ability. It is a cheap device to elicit sympathy. Talking about himself, the speaker actually obstructs the cause he seeks to advance by suggesting that his own comfort is first in importance.

Is This Trip Necessary ?

Imagine yourself primed for the climax of a great convention at Atlantic City. As the president of a large steel corporation begins to speak, you measure his words against your recent journey of three thousand miles, and you find yourself asking, "Was this trip necessary?" Here is the beginning of the speech that prompts such a disquieting query:

"Ladies and Gentlemen:

"You can sense the embarrassment that I feel in following the very distinguished address from that great American who is now president of Johns Hopkins University.

"I have the feeling that if I am remembered at all after you have returned to your homes, it will be as the man who spoiled an otherwise good afternoon.

"I am a little embarrassed that you have been given the subject of my address. I am bound to say that if there is anything in what I say that resembles my title, it will be purely coincidental.

"It is a great privilege for me to be here . . . ."

Apology and excuse-making are in bad taste before any audience. Either do the job the best you can without reference to yourself, unless it is pertinent to the subject or occasion, or don't speak. Don't add to the plague of distasteful speech openings. Use the positive devices stressed in this volume for securing interest, and you will be gratified by the improved response of your audience.

A Moment of Rapt Attention

Remember, a *good* introduction brings the minds of the audience together by arousing curiosity and suspense. It leads the listeners eagerly and naturally into the speech and points ahead to the discussion itself.

The purpose of the following introductions from actual addresses is to show how to use suggestion constructively in beginning your speeches.

Visualize the speaker as he arises. He pauses while all faces turn toward him. For a moment he possesses undivided attention. All are waiting to discover what kind of speaker is about to address them. They will soon know. His first words and manner will tell them.

Illustration

"A few years ago a Cleveland hospital was destroyed by fire. One of the physicians who ministered to its victims was himself overcome by gas. When he realized that he was dying, he said to his wife, as if in justification of the risk he had taken, 'My dear, these people must be cared for.'

"Today the victims of a terrible depression *must* be cared for. Through no fault of their own they have lost their jobs. However capable and reliable, they are unable to find jobs. They are just as truly the victims of a great calamity as are people who are left homeless by a hurricane, a flood, or an earthquake. Can we allow them to go hungry? Not so long as we ourselves have enough to eat and to spare! Can we allow them to be without shelter in winter weather? Not so long as we ourselves have a bed to sleep in and a roof over our heads! 'These people must be cared for.' Why? Because we who are acquainted with their need are something more than the beasts of the field that allow their kind to suffer and die unattended. We have become sufficiently human to be humane.'"*

Quotation

"In the line of the "Ancient Mariner," Coleridge has left etched on the memories of the English-speaking world the figure of a ship becalmed under a blistering sun. By the magic of the author's words we can almost see the sails hanging limp, the deck seared by the heat, the sailors waiting wistfully for the wind that does not come. And we can veritably feel the parch in the throat when we read the lines, 'Water, water, everywhere but not a drop to drink.'

"This line suggests to me a modern paraphrase. After two world wars we thought we were surely launched on the voyage to a world of peace and brotherhood. But we seem to be tragically halted. At the same time we see power almost immeasurably multiplied. Mechanical power has been advanced by our dynamic industrial efficiency, and now atomic energy gives a throbbing new sense of potency. Hence we could say: power, power, everywhere and yet no strength to save us. Paradoxically we are becalmed on a sea of power."†

---

* Dr. Ernest F. Tittle in a talk before a community group.

† Dr. Ralph W. Sockman, "The Worth of One" in *Vital Speeches*, Volume XV, Number 21.

Humorous Anecdote

"Two Irishmen landed in New York. They had not been around very much, so they decided to take a train trip. As they were riding along, a boy came through selling fruit. They recognized oranges and apples, but there was a strange fruit they had never seen before so they asked the boy, 'What is that?'

"He answered, 'That is a banana.'

" 'Is it good to eat?'

"He said, 'Sure.'

" 'How do you eat it?'

"The boy showed them how to peel a banana, so each bought one. One fellow took a bite out of his, and just then the train went into a tunnel.

"He said, 'Great heavens, Pat, if you haven't eaten the darned thing, don't do it. I ate mine, and I've gone blind.'

"Very frequently we get fixed ideas about organized labor and what organized labor is thinking . . . . We do not think of analyzing the motives behind some of the things we read about in the newspapers or some of the things people say. Like the two Irishmen, we see only the result, without looking for the cause. If we would look beyond the result to the cause, we would observe that in dealing with these problems we need an understanding of human relationships."*

Startling Statement

"A member of a certain Middle West legislature sought an appropriation of $100,000 for the protection of public

---

* Adapted from a speech by Cyrus S. Ching entitled, "The Future of Labor-Management Relations," in *Vital Speeches*, Volume XV, Number 19.

health; but could secure only $5,000. One morning he put upon the desk of each legislator before the opening of the session, a fable which ran something like this: A sick mother with a baby is told by a physician that she has tuberculosis and that she should seek a higher altitude. Lack of means prevents her going. She applies to the government and is told that not a dollar is available to save the mother and her child from death. At the same time a farmer observes that one of his hogs has cholera symptoms. He sends a telegram, collect, to the government. An inspector comes next day, treats the hog with serum and cures it. Moral: *Be a hog!*"*

Rhetorical Question

"Mr. President and Members of the Holland Society:

"Who is the typical Dutchman? Rembrandt, the splendid artist; Erasmus, the brilliant scholar; Coster, the inventor of printing; Leuwenhoek, the profound scientist; Grotius, the great lawyer; Barendz, the daring explorer; De Witt, the skillful statesman; Van Tromp, the trump of admirals; William the Silent, heroic defender of liberty against a world of tyranny; William III, the emancipator of England, whose firm, peaceful hand, just two centuries ago, set the Anglo-Saxon race free to fulfill its mighty destiny — what hero, artist, philosopher, discoverer, lawgiver, admiral, general or monarch shall we choose from the long list of Holland's illustrious dead to stand as the typical Dutchman?

"Nay, not one of these men, famous as they were, can fill the pedestal of honor tonight. For though their glorious

---

* Quoted in James A. Winans, *Public Speaking*, p. 209, The Century Company, New York. 1923. Reprinted by permission.

achievements have lent an undying luster to the name of Holland, the qualities that made Holland great were the qualities of the common people."*

References to Subject or Problem

"What some people call the two-billion dollar question: 'Can man learn to control the machines he has created?' has been eloquently sketched by Fitzpatrick, the great cartoonist of the St. Louis *Post Dispatch*. He has drawn a vast bomb leaning against a wall, beside it an equally tall question mark. Two little men in the foreground are looking up at the huge monoliths. The bomb is labelled: 'How to kill everybody,' and the other: 'How to live with everybody.'

"I would like to tell you about my experiences in recent years trying to explore that question mark. *What dependable knowledge is now available on how to live with everybody?* How far has the science of human relations progressed since Alexander Pope observed in a famous poem that the proper study of mankind is man? We know enough about the behavior of atoms to dissolve considerable sections of the planet. What do we know about the behavior of people in groups and societies?"†

Reference to Occasion

"It is always a pleasure to come to Alabama, and especially do I welcome this opportunity to address the Bar Association of this great Southern State. I firmly believe

---

* Henry van Dyke, "The Typical Dutchman," in *Modern Eloquence*, III, 363. Lincoln Scholarship Fund Edition, New York. 1928.

† Stuart Chase, "The Proper Study of Mankind," in *Vital Speeches*, Volume XV. Number 17.

that the lawyers of the country, perhaps more than any other group, are keenly aware of what is going on in this great land of ours toward destruction of Constitutional government. As lawyers, and as members of the Alabama Bar, you are deeply concerned with the preservation of our democratic processes, of which you are a vital part. I feel certain that the message I bring you today will fall upon sympathetic ears."*

Concluding the Speech

The speaker should conclude his speech within the time set for his part of the program. Under no circumstances should he extend his remarks.†

As a safeguard against stealing someone else's time or prolonging the meeting, the speaker should not try to cover too much ground. He should limit his specific purpose to include only that which he can comfortably develop.

Whoa There !

Too many speakers act as if they were trying to exhaust both subject and audience. How the defenseless listener reacts against a drawn-out speech is related by Mark Twain. He said: "Some years ago in Hartford, we all went to church one hot, sweltering night to hear the annual report of Mr. Hawley, a city missionary who went around finding people who needed help and didn't want to ask for it.

"He told of the life in cellars, where poverty resided; he gave instances of heroism and devotion of the poor.

---

* J. Strom Thurmond, "O'er the Ramparts We Watch," in *Vital Speeches*, Volume XVI, Number 1.

† For methods of developing the discussion, see Chapters VIII, X, XI, and XIII.

'When a man with millions gives,' he said, 'we make a great deal of noise. It's noise in the wrong place, for it's the widow's mite that counts.'

"Well, Hawley worked me up to great pitch. I could hardly wait for him to get through. I had $400 in my pocket. I wanted to give that and borrow more to give. You could see greenbacks in every eye. But instead of passing the plate then, he kept on talking and talking, and as he talked it grew hotter and hotter, and we grew sleepier

and sleepier. My enthusiasm went down, down, down — $100 at a clip — until finally when the plate did come around, I stole ten cents out of it. It all goes to show how a little thing like this can lead to crime."*

Time Is of the Essence

To drive an audience to desperation, the night does not have to be hot — the speech and meeting need only to be too long. Mark Twain portrays how enthusiasm and

* *Thesaurus of Anecdotes*, edited by Edmund Fuller, pp. 58-59. Crown Publishers, New York. 1942.

good resolution can rapidly diminish. Long-winded speeches cause resentment and reduce assimilation by the audience. Prominence and reputation for eloquence should not deceive a speaker into believing that he can disregard this fact. Stop while the listeners would like to hear more.

The Final Cadence

To run out of material finally and stop by saying, "I guess that's all," "I suppose I've covered the subject," or "I think I've said enough," is a poor way of concluding a speech. Another equally poor device is to say, "I thank you!" These trite words divert the attention of the listeners from the strength of what you may have said to your own ingratiating manner.

A strong conclusion will result from the application of similar techniques used in a good introduction. The method selected must fulfill one function. It must focus the thinking and feeling of the audience upon the specific purpose developed in the discussion. It must leave a well-defined impression in the mind of the listener.

Ending a speech is not alone a matter of *what* is said, but also *how* it is said. A speech must sound finished and avoid halting, hesitating manner, and uncertain tone. The concluding words must ring down the curtain with finality. Use these time-tested, effective ways of ending your talk:

> Summarize.
>
> Issue a challenge.
>
> Make an appeal.
>
> Use an illustration.

Cite a quotation.

Read a poem.

Re-echo the message.

Dramatize the point.

Paint a picture.*

Remember, it isn't a complete absence of faults but the presence of many virtues that make for effective speaking.

Keep before you the suggestions given by the early Greek teachers of rhetoric:

"Stand up in order that you may be seen;

Speak up in order that you may be heard;

Shut up in order that you may be appreciated!"

---

* Some of these methods have been illustrated in this volume already: The Challenge or Appeal in "Don't Die On Third!" p. 132; The Quotation in "Emerson is Right," p. 137 and in "Socialized Medicine," p. 143; Summary or Recapitulation in "How to Live a Hundred Years Happily!" p. 150.

(See pp. 180-81 for chart on how to develop the
three divisions of a speech.)

How to Develop the Three Divisions of a Speech

```
┌─────────────────────────┐
│  GENERAL PURPOSE         │
│  SPECIFIC PURPOSE        │
└─────────────────────────┘
```

(Limit scope of specific purpose so you can cover material in time allotted without being sketchy. Never try to include too much in a speech.)

Introduction

Purpose:

To gain attention.

To arouse interest.

To secure good will for both speaker and subject.

To state your subject.

To supply background information.

To suggest speech purpose.

To make a brief and logical transition into discussion.

Do this by:

Arousing curiosity and suspense.

Telling audience how to get what it wants.

Discussion or Body
Main Ideas I, II, and III

(There may be more or less than three main ideas in a talk. Three or four, however, are usually sufficient. Develop each as outlined below.)

Purpose of discussion or body:

Achieve general purpose.

Emphasize specific purpose and main theme.

Elaborate and develop main ideas and leading points.

Hold attention, interest, and sympathy of audience throughout speech.

Do this by:

Stating your main points.

Restating them in different ways.

Conclusion or Ending

Purpose:

Re-focus thinking and feeling of audience upon specific purpose.

Restate main ideas.

Clinch specific purpose.

Appeal for action.

Arouse enthusiasm.

Do this by:

Re-echoing the argument and thought of entire talk through apt illustration, quotation, or poem, etc.

Starting with a situation.
Stating an idea that makes a difference.
Using narrative-descriptive opening.
Beginning with an effect needing a cause or vice versa.
"Yes" response from audience to acceptable ideas.
Presenting a conflict.
Using the:
Factual or imaginary illustration.
Quotation of prose or poem.
Humorous anecdote.
Shock technique or startling statement.
Rhetorical question.
Reference to subject or problem.
Reference to occasion.
Literary opening.
Personal greeting.
But . . .
Do not apologize or make excuses.

Presenting reasons.
Applying a principle.
Stating cause and effect.
Inducing an imagined experience for the listener through vivid imagery.
Using:
Illustrations.
Specific examples.
Humorous and human interest stories.
Definition.
Particulars and details.
Dramatized statistics.
Comparisons and contrasts.
Analogies and figures of speech.
Quotations.
Competent testimony by authority.
Facts and figures.
Fables, parables, and poems.
Cumulation and repetition.
Four forms of discourse:
Narration, description, exposition, argumentation or persuasion.
Visual Aids: Charts, maps, diagrams, cartoons, blackboard, actual material, exhibits.

Using a vivid dramatization.
Making a strong and impelling recapitulation or summary.
Visualizing the objective so vividly that audience feels overwhelmingly in the situation. Doing this is the surest way to persuading listeners.
Giving warnings.
Announcing your own personal intentions.
Appealing for action through basic drives.

Tie all divisions of speech together through transitions and connectives.
Give speech unity, coherence, and emphasis.

CHAPTER XV

CUES FOR YOU

"HE WHO never quotes, is never quoted," said Charles H. Spurgeon, gifted English preacher. This was his way of emphasizing that appropriate quotations are precious to you as a speaker. They enable you to produce an effect much the same as if you had brought an authority to the platform with you to add his word in support of your idea, or a bard or man of letters to endow it with beauty and appeal.

Quote Experts for Endorsement

Observe how J. Strom Thurmond, Governor of South Carolina, builds the conclusion of his address entitled, "O'er the Ramparts We Watched!" with a quotation from George Washington. His style makes unnecessary the use of those trite words, *quote* and *unquote*:

"Let us remember our glorious heritage . . . . Let us take courage, as Washington did when he replied to General Howe's assertion that the American cause was lost.

"General Washington declared, 'For myself, I'd have lied within if I surrendered. The spirit of liberty moves over earth like flame, and finds fresh home when the old's burned out. It stands over this, my country, in this dark year, and is a pillar of fire to show us an uncouth clan, a dream that men shall walk upright, masterless, doff hat to none, and choose their gods.'

"So said Washington. And in this hour, his 'flame of liberty' is spreading still.

"Let us, like Washington, watch 'o'er the ramparts,' and let us keep our beloved country forever 'the land of the free.' "

In this same address, Governor Thurmond used other quotations to reinforce his point that we must resist the encroachment of the federal government upon our liberties. He cited the ancient Greek historian, Polybius, on what happens to the citizens of a nation when they are captivated by the wiles of faithless leaders who beguile them into becoming "habituated to feed at the expense of others, and to have their hope of livelihood in the property of their neighbors." Polybius also said: "They are made ready and greedy to receive bribes, and the virtue of the democracy is destroyed, and it is transformed into a goverment of violence and the strong hand." In the development of his central idea, Governor Thurmond also quoted Webster, Wilson, Jefferson, Madison, Justice Roberts, Dean Roscoe Pound, Senator Borah, and others, as well as the Constitution itself.*

The listeners accepted these distinguished gentlemen because of their knowledge, experience, and integrity. Materials from such sources are especially helpful to overcome doubt, indifference, and hostility. Hence, the speaker quotes scholars in the arts and sciences, generals and admirals on warfare, doctors on medicine and health, and the Scriptures in support of religious doctrine.

Quote Poetic Gems

Quotations have aesthetic value in addition to their efficacy as testimony. A few lines from a poem, a choice

---

* J. Strom Thurmond, "O'er the Ramparts We Watched," in *Vital Speeches*, Volume XVI, Number 1.

bit from the writing of a philosopher, or an apt folk expression may restate the speaker's thought in an impressive and inspiring manner. In a talk emphasizing that no one is too small to play an important role, Mr. Bradshaw Mintener skillfully weaves a poetic gem into the fabric of his speech:

"Suppose — just suppose — that God were to tap you on the shoulder and say, 'Whom shall I send?' Did I say suppose? We need not suppose, for He is doing just that every day of our lives. And the very fact He does it is evidence enough to indicate that He thinks there is something each one of us can do. Begin doing it — now.

" 'I am only one,
But I am one.
I cannot do everything,
But I can do something.
What I can do,
I ought to do;
And what I ought to do,
By the grace of God, I will do.'

"There is something that you and I can do to be and become Better Men. Let us determine to do it 'By the grace of God' for Better Times. Think of the thrill you will enjoy when you can say, 'Here am I, send me. I am one of the Better Men wanted for Better Times.' "*

Read Radiantly

As a speaker, you will frequently find it useful to read to an audience from the printed page. You should aim to

---

* Bradshaw Mintener, "Wanted — Better Men for Better Times," quoting Harold W. Ruopp, in *Vital Speeches*, Volume XV, Number 10.

carry to your listeners completeness of meaning so vividly that the author's intention is recreated. You should give the impression that you are wide-awake and interested in what you are reading and that you believe it to be worthy of the attention of your hearers.

In achieving these objectives, the following suggestions will serve as a useful guide:

1. Make every reasonable preparation. Type your quotation on a card and, for readability, double space it. Then read it aloud at frequent intervals.

2. Do not flounder on words you can't pronounce. For proper names refer to the back of Webster's *Collegiate Dictionary* where there are sections entitled "A Pronouncing Gazetteer" and "Pronouncing Biographical Dictionary." Funk and Wagnalls and Winston and several other dictionaries include this material in the main section. Write into your notes the phonetic spelling of any word that may cause you to stumble.

3. Understand the total effect of what you read. Search out background materials concerning the author and selection. Then, underscore key words and phrases. Mark places that you wish to give special stress or at points where you wish to pause. This preparation is your best insurance for effective oral reading.

4. Read ideas rather than mere words. Practice until you can glance at your notes, get the meaning of an entire sentence or two, and talk with your audience as if the material were your own. This is the secret of communicativeness in oral reading. In order to keep the

place, move the thumb of the hand in which you are holding your notes to the line where you are reading.

5. Grasp the drama in your quotation and portray it for your listeners. See Socrates as he heroically imbibes his hemlock cup; shiver with Washington's army at Valley Forge; hear the voice of the aged Franklin speak faith and wisdom before the Constitutional Convention. Project yourself into both the intellectual and emotional content of what you read. This will enable your voice to respond with inflections that are meaningful. It will enable you to pause in the right places and to speak at an intelligible rate with expressive volume and pitch. Grasp of the drama will help you to overcome the commonest of all faults — reading too rapidly and mechanically.

6. Keep your inflection from falling downward except to express completeness of thought and for emphasis. The pitch should never fall within phrases and between subject and verb. To avoid jerkiness, phrase your thought in word groups consistent with the meaning. The fewer the breaks within the idea the better.

7. Control the mechanics of reading. Never play with your notes. See that there is a stand where you can keep them except when you are actually reading. Check on such items as the lighting, the microphone, the heat, and the ventilation before you speak.

8. Take ample time when you read orally. As the phrases come filing past the windows of your mind, ask yourself continually, "Do I know the meaning?" and, "What is this idea worth?" Find enjoyment in reading aloud, both in practice and before listeners.

Make Friends with the Mike

In the "good old days" the speaker had to be all lungs and the audience all ears. Those days are gone. The microphone is here. Take advantage of its benefits, and you will find it to be a helpful ally instead of a gadget to push aside.

At meetings of a service club in the ballroom of a metropolitan hotel, the uninitiated speaker often arises, looks at the public address system, and shouts, "I'm sure I don't need this thing!" Then some outspoken member of the group generally yells back, "Use it, brother, use it!" And he is right. Such a system was put there because at least in some parts of the room people have difficulty in hearing. Here are a few simple suggestions that will help you make friends with the mike:

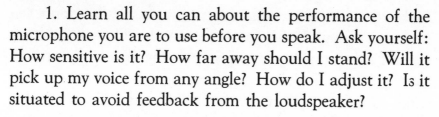

1. Learn all you can about the performance of the microphone you are to use before you speak. Ask yourself: How sensitive is it? How far away should I stand? Will it pick up my voice from any angle? How do I adjust it? Is it situated to avoid feedback from the loudspeaker?

You may have to regulate the height of the mike while you are talking. To fumble and twist or have to summon help is distressing for you and the audience. Your listeners want to be able to see your face and eyes, so don't have the mike too high — chin or chest level is better than face level. Discipline yourself to stand at a constant distance from it while you are speaking. This will avoid having the sound blast the eardrums one moment and die away the next.

For your own protection, have someone that knows his business handle the volume controls. These precautions are important to your success as a speaker.

2. Speak into the microphone as you would into the telephone. When using the telephone, you talk to the person listening at the other end. You don't talk to the mouthpiece, nor are you in the least conscious of the instrument itself. In an auditorium do the same: talk to your listeners, not to the mike. It is merely the avenue through which you reach them more pleasantly and intimately.

3. Remember that the microphone amplifies everything — the bad as well as the good. Don't rattle notes or papers or make remarks not intended for the listener. Don't over-articulate sounds such as "s," "p," or "b." Beware of over-preciseness and affectation, and be especially careful to avoid slovenliness and bad pronunciation. The microphone magnifies these, too.

4. Control the quality of your voice. The microphone makes voice strain or distortion unnecessary, so don't yell and don't pound the speaker's stand. The microphone doesn't adjust quickly to sudden blasting, booming, rattling, or sputtering. Ease into difficult sounds and louder volume. Check the pitch of your voice so it will not rumble in the back of your throat or rise to a squeaky treble. Use a great deal of variety within a limited range. Speak out clearly, expressively, and thoughtfully. Speak deliberately, especially in large auditoriums, so that the echo of one word doesn't distort the clarity of another.

5. Keep your hands off the microphone and stand. The writer once heard a recording of a speech and wondered what it was that sounded like pounding steampipes. He

was told that the speaker had caressed the microphone throughout his talk.

Airing Your Speech

You may have an opportunity to talk over the radio. The experience will be valuable. Take it! Apply the suggestions already made in this chapter about reading aloud before the microphone. Studios usually require a manuscript, so here is the occasion to write a speech that occupies an exact period of time. Observe the principles of illustration and arrangement as already discussed and deliver your talk in a direct, conversational style.* Speak intimately with three or four people. Forget the thousands who may be listening. It may help you to have several of your friends seated before you in the studio to achieve this personal relationship. Since you will not be seen by your radio audience, your voice must carry the full load of delivery. Use gestures if they will help you feel alive and communicative. Ask the announcer to instruct you about going on and off the air and to give you any other useful pointers.

Toastmaster or Roastmaster ?

The writer has attended many programs where the chairman or toastmaster acted as if he were expected to crack an indefinite number of dull and meatless jokes. Nothing gives the audience more pain. One of many such instances comes to mind. There were four preliminary speakers and a principal speaker on the program of a flower club. The toastmaster had collected forty jokes and wisecracks from three popular publications. He had them piled

---

* See "Don't Die on Third," p. 132, for an example of an effective speech delivered over the radio.

up in front of him just as he had clipped them from the magazines. In an appropriate situation, a selected few of these "gems," well-told and tied in with an intelligent plan  for the evening's entertainment, would have been excellent; but in such pointless and badly delivered profusion, they were like yesterday's faded flowers. A few straggling, forced laughs formed the tepid response of the audience to this artless "roastmaster." The results were dismal. When the principal speaker was finally presented, the meeting had already run an hour beyond schedule, and everyone was wilted.

The effect was much like that produced by the chairman who arose and said, "I realize that you would much rather be listening to this interesting program than to me. . . . But I *am* reminded of a story — which you have probably all heard.

"It seems that there were two Irishmen walking down the street when they came to a . . . oh, I should have said in the first place that the parrot was hanging out in *front* of the store . . . or rather belonging to one of these two fellows . . . the *first* Irishman, that is . . . was . . . . well, *anyway*, this parrot . . ."* and so on to the bitter end. Don't do it! If you have a chance to be chairman, toastmaster, or after-dinner speaker, don't follow such a foolish routine. Use imagination, study the occasion, and determine what

---

* Robert Benchley, in A *Treasury of Laughter*, p. 38, edited by Louis Untermeyer. Simon and Schuster, New York. 1946. Reprinted by permission.

is expected. Make a plan and inject freshness and vitality into it. The effective chairman or speaker will avoid doing and expressing what most other individuals would do and express on the same occasion. He will be original and will surprise his audience. But he will be certain that his remarks are relevant, directing attention to the purpose of the gathering and not to his own originality. Some standards for your performance on these occasions follow:

If you have a program to plan, select a theme and choose speakers that will fit it, or select a speaker and build your program around him. Unless you are absolutely sure of the ability of your speaker, remember that several short talks are better than a long dull one. Have the best speaker talk last.

If you are unknown to the audience, get yourself introduced before you take the program over. Start on time and close on time. Allow a definite number of minutes for each event and stick to a predetermined timetable. Tell each speaker in advance both how long he is to talk and in what manner you are going to notify him that his time is up.

Make certain that your speaker knows all the important facts about his audience and the occasion. Inject good feeling into your manner; be alive; create an atmosphere of enjoyment with a bit of appropriate humor, if you can; but remember that your principal job is not to be funny but to see that the program moves along smoothly and on schedule. See that your guests, rather than you, are in the limelight. This doesn't require great talent, just common sense, imagination, and planning.

Topping the Dessert

If you are to be an after-dinner speaker and you want to be remembered longer than the menu, observe these suggestions:

1. Plan your talk. Give it unity of thought. Any series of items you may present should hang together on one central idea. You might follow this procedure: Tell an anecdote, story, personal experience, illustration, or read a poem. Then point out the theme or main idea around which you are going to unify the details of your speech. Next, follow with a number of additional personal experiences, anecdotes, or illustrations that strengthen and amplify your purpose. Arrange the material so as to create a balance between humor and human interest. Save one of your strongest anecdotes for the conclusion. Finally, make a striking restatement of your main idea. Some serious sentiment should underlie your fun. Tie it into your theme as you finish.*

2. Get off to a good start. Avoid saying, "Your chairman's remarks remind me of a story . . . ." A good deal of the charm of a story lies in having it sprung upon your listeners unexpectedly.

3. Employ humor wisely as a "change of pace," along with a touch of pathos or an illustrative story. Audiences yearn for contrast during a talk.

4. Have a *reason* for telling an anecdote.

5. Build your stories around well-known personalities and local situations. Never let your anecdotes sound like something out of a joke book.

---

* See Chapters IX and XI for other methods of developing and arranging your material.

6. Keep your story moving. Come to the point quickly. The more complicated and involved it is, the more likely the point will be obscured. Avoid dialect unless you can do it well.

7. Be thoroughly familiar with your anecdote and avoid laughing at it, but don't wear an expression on your face that implies that you'd be hurt if someone else laughed.

8. Pause just before you speak the "gag" or "cracker" line and express it so that everyone will get it. Deliver it with increased verve, animation, and interpretative gestures. Dramatize it!

A Cue from Churchill

This is a chapter of cues for you who are striving to improve your speaking ability. If you need a little encouragement to apply them, remember that perfection is not spelled with ten letters, but with eight — p-r-a-c-t-i-c-e !

Winston Churchill declared: "According to the newspapers, I am supposed to be quite a good speaker — indeed, I am sometimes called an orator and all that. The truth is that . . . I only learned to speak, somehow or other, with exceptional difficulty and *enormous practice.* I have never persevered in anything as I have in trying to convey my thoughts and feelings forcefully and easily, convincingly and persuasively, to my fellow men."

CHAPTER XVI

THOUGHT ON FIRE

The Quick . . .

VICTOR HUGO, French author, delivered an address commemorating the one-hundredth anniversary of Voltaire's death. At the time, the speaker himself was over seventy-six years of age. Colonel Thomas W. Higginson, American man of letters, heard Hugo speak and observed that he neither memorized nor read his address. He spoke from notes in immense handwriting.

The speaker was spontaneous and alive. Higginson describes his delivery and its effect upon the audience: "He used much gesture, and in impassioned moments he waved his arm above his head, the fingers apart and trembling with emotion. Sometimes he clapped one hand to his head as if to tear out some of his white hairs, though this hardly seemed, at the moment, melodramatic. . . . Never was there a more powerful picture than his sketch of 'that frightful international exposition called a field of battle.' "*

. . . and the Dead

Contrast the electrifying delivery of Victor Hugo with the inert manner of Matthew Arnold, distinguished English poet and literary critic. Because of his renown, he was

---

* *Modern Eloquence*, IX, 265. Lincoln Scholarship Fund Edition, New York. 1928.

brought to America for a series of lectures. In New York City, the house was sold out for his first address. People stood in the aisles in great expectation. Major J. B. Pond, in his lecture, "Memories of the Lyceum," relates that when the eloquent Chauncey Depew con-  cluded his introduction of the speaker: "Matthew Arnold step- ped forward, opened out his man- uscript, laid it on the desk, and his lips began to move. There was not the slightest sound audible from where I stood. After a few minutes General Grant said to Mrs. Grant, 'Well, wife, we have paid to see the British lion; we cannot hear him roar, so we had better go home.' They left the hall. A few minutes later there was a stream of people leaving the place. All those standing went away early. Later on, the others who could not endure the silence moved away as quietly as they could."*

Arnold's dismal, boring performance was repeated one hundred times. It was a tragedy that one gifted in so many ways should prove himself inept in telling others what he knew.

A Call for Action !

Vitality and action would have helped Mr. Arnold. If he had abandoned his manuscript and talked from his vast knowledge, his lecture could not have been so stifling. On this point Beecher proclaimed: "The most successful

---

* *Modern Eloquence*, XIII, 335-36. Lincoln Scholarship Fund Edition, New York. 1928.

speakers are men of great vitality and force; men who have pre-eminently the explosive power by which they can thrust their materials out. They are catapults, and men go down before them."

Demosthenes, when asked, "What is the chief part of an orator?" answered, "Action." "What next?" "Action." "What next again?" "ACTION !" Cicero, another of the ancient orators, declared that without action great oratorical gifts are lost; with it, the mediocre speaker can surpass genius itself. "Action," he asserted, "is a kind of physical eloquence." And Quintilian stressed that "For my own part, I would not hesitate to assert that a mediocre speech supported by all the power of delivery will be more impressive than the best speech unaccompanied by such power."

Listen to the provincial "reader" quote Shakespeare in contrast to the intrepretation of a great actor. One flickers like the lightning bug; the other blazes like a flash of lightning. Garrick, the famous English actor of the eighteenth century, said he would give a small fortune if he could project, "Oh," as could one of his rivals. A friend of the notorious Mirabeau of the French Revolution complained that the citizens would not listen to him. Mirabeau went before their assembly with the identical words and inflamed their will to act. It is reported that "The words were the same; the fire that made them thrilling and electric were not his friend's, but his own."

Bury Your Inhibitions

To achieve the kind of speaking power demonstrated by Hugo, Mirabeau, and other notables, one speech expert asserts that "inhibitions and repressions must be removed," and explains that "many individuals appear dull . . . because excessive timidity . . . or habitual repression of feeling makes it . . . impossible for them to express what is taking place within themselves . . . .

"Whatever the fundamental causes, repressive tendencies must be broken down if . . . either a good voice or an effective personality is to be fully realized. This development must be kept within reasonable bounds, of course; no one admires the impulsive, unpredictable, completely uninhibited person who, though he may be the 'life of the party,' is rash and extravagant in his speech and behavior generally. Such behavior suggests insincerity and instability. For the average person, however, this is more a theoretical than an actual danger; what his speech most needs is more spontaneity and versatility of expression."*

For the person who is free from restraint and self-consciousness, nothing is more natural than to gesture.

Thought and gesture should be one. William Jennings Bryan was welcomed by audiences everywhere because he was an active and vigorous speaker. But listeners, when questioned, could not remember that he gestured at all. His words and action said the same thing. The key to Bryan's success as a speaker is indicated by himself in his lecture on "The Spoken Word." He said: "Eloquence may be defined as the speech of one who *knows what he is talking about* and *means what he says — it is thought on fire!*"†

The best speakers are more than mere voices; they speak with their whole bodies and with all their resources

---

* Virgil A. Anderson, *Training the Speaking Voice*, p. 221. Oxford University Press, New York. 1942. Reprinted by permission.

† *Modern Eloquence*, XIII, 92. Lincoln Scholarship Fund Edition, New York. 1928.

of mind, spirit, and feeling. Inaction and sameness in delivery serve as a monotonous lullaby that puts the listeners to sleep. The rule should be: When the audience dozes, don't disturb the sleepers; prod the speaker!

Let the Whole Man Speak

Here is a summary of why purposeful action should be developed and used by all speakers:

1. Action increases the speaker's metabolism and releases his energy for communication. (This is not to be confused with mere fidgeting, however, which wastes strength and eats up the speaker's vitality.)

2. Action enables the speaker to achieve poise, which is the right balance between tension and relaxation.

3. Action uses the muscles and helps the speaker overcome fear of appearing in public. Most of the things man does well are accomplished with his *whole body* working as a unit. Good gestures involve all the body muscles from the toes to the top of the head.

4. Action helps the speaker remember his ideas and promotes fluency. Since, as some contend, the "mind is what the body is doing," there is a definite relationship between free bodily movement and rhythmical, fluent speech. "Tie a Frenchmen's hands, and he cannot speak."

5. Action arouses empathy in the listener. *Sympathy* is a "feeling with," but *empathy* is a "feeling into." Empathy involves a muscular response from the listener. People project themselves into situations which they observe. They tense muscles of legs and

back during a football game or race. An audience
tends to respond to every movement of the speaker.
This enables the speaker to stir up meaning in his
hearers and is important because meanings themselves cannot be transferred from one mind to another; only the symbols that evoke them can be
communicated. The power of oratory lies in the
ears, the eyes, and the muscles of the listeners as
well as in the tongue of the speaker.

6. Action stimulates audience interest and holds attention. We'd rather watch a motion picture than a
still one. Similarly, we are attracted to the active
speaker rather than to the quiet one.

7. Action helps the audience visualize the speaker's
ideas as he portrays location, size, shape, importance, and dramatic elements.

First the Gesture

Our understanding of gesture can be made clearer by
an examination of its origin. Dr. Kimball Young points out
that all "language has its roots in gestures," and that speech
itself "is nothing else but a form of vocal gesture." If we
are "to understand the foundations of language," explains
Dr. Young, "it is necessary to see it in terms of the evolution
of the whole gesture system — vocal, manual, and facial."*

The use of gesture is revealed in the culture of many
peoples and further emphasizes the tremendous significance
it plays in conveying meaning:

---

* *Social Psychology*, p. 204. F. S. Crofts and Co., New York. 1930. Reprinted by permission.

The Chinese dramatists have long depended upon stereotyped gestures to convey ideas. A slight spreading of the hands, for example, indicates the opening of a door.

Ceasar, by turning thumbs down, gave his victorious gladiators the right to partake of the glories of victory and to kill their victims. This gesture still signifies contempt or finality.

Tribes of American Indians, using different languages, were able to communicate with one another by a universal sign language that consisted entirely of gesture. Deaf-mutes use a highly conventionalized system of gestures. It is based upon the spoken language, however, and substitutes gestures for the letters of words. Soldiers are often trained to use formalized gestures when the noise of battle prevents communication by sound.

The traveler in a foreign land may be forced to resort to gestures. It is surprising how effectively one can converse in gesture alone.*

Gesture lies at the roots of our written and spoken language. In early Egypt, for example, many disagreements

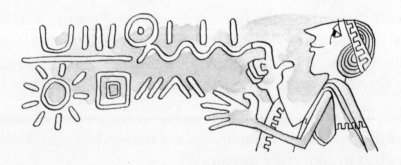

---

* The facts about the use of gestures are from Richard T. LaPiere and Paul R. Farnsworth, *Social Psychology*, p. 72. McGraw-Hill Book Co., Inc., New York. 1942. Used by permission.

arose over how much grain one farmer owed another. Memory was fickle, and some system of accounting had to be devised. The gesture used to accompany speech, when the farmer talked about a basket, was scratched into a picture on the rough mud walls of his house. This meant one basket of grain was either borrowed or lent. Next to the picture of the basket, straight lines in a row were added to count the number of baskets involved in the transaction —

Other pictures were drawn to record additional meanings and experiences. The sun was a circle with a dot in the center —⊙. Water was three or four waves —〰.

Then the scholars among the people of Egypt went further. They "began to combine several drawings to indicate words of which they could make no pictures. They could not, for example, draw a picture to mean *understand*." But they had gestures to portray agreement, just as we do when we talk with one another. These they scratched into pictures. If two feet 𐤔 always meant *stand*, and the picture sign of gateway ⌐ always meant *under*, "by placing the two signs together ⌐𐤔 they had a simple drawing which clearly meant *understand*."*

Look at these picture symbols and you will see that, old as they are, they still represent the gestures you make with your hands when you talk about a basketful of grain, the hot sun in the sky, the waves that roll onto the beach, or the fact that you understand.

---

* Adapted from Olive B. Miller, A *Picturesque Tale of Progress*, I, 81. The Book House for Children, Chicago. 1935. Used by permission.

Gestures Enhance Meaning

The language of gesture, so important to early civilization, still adds to the meaning of the spoken word. Not only is this obvious to the casual observer; but it is also a decisive factor as reported in scientific studies. Professors LaPiere and Farnsworth of Stanford University state: "Under ordinary circumstances, gestures are a supplement to words, enriching them and giving the hearer something to look at while he listens. They may even change the communication value of words or phrases — a fact that is reflected in the common admonition, *'Smile when you say that!'* "

Further, they say, gestures often supplement and modify the "effects of the spoken word" and in reality "provide a much more subtle means of communication than does speech" itself.

These authors submit the following case as typical of their findings: "At one time, the overflow from a class in one of our larger universities was put in a well-proctored second room which was equipped for radio reception. While the instructor lectured directly to the students of the original class, only his voice via the microphone came to those in the second room. The overflow students could hear almost perfectly, but they had no speaker on whom to fix attention. They seemed ill at ease; the predominant posture soon adopted was that of resting the head upon the hand." The measured learning of the overflow group averaged lower than that of the students who both heard and saw the instructor.

LaPiere and Farnsworth explain that gestures "can be used with deliberate effort to influence others. Some of the most spectacular public speakers depend almost as much upon posture, movement of hands, and facial expression as upon speech to obtain their effects. Some, in fact, seem to depend almost wholly upon gesture."*

Conviction Is the Mainspring of Action

To make a speech convincing, the inner spirit of the speaker must burn hot and radiate its warmth in spontaneous gesture. The effective speaker never resorts to artificial effects. For him and his audience, stagey gesticulation is repugnant. He is deeply and earnestly sincere. He knows that no gesture is honest unless it expresses a genuine feeling from deep down inside himself.

In many instances, a sincere speaker fails to communicate because he mumbles as though talking primarily to himself. He must get "steamed-up" and convert his energy into bodily action.

Readiness to speak requires much more of the speaker than merely organizing materials around a central idea. It involves an emotional preparation as well. Some speakers restrict themselves to an intellectual preparation only. To this degree, they narrow communication to those meanings conveyed by words alone. They are like a hammer without an arm — powerless to drive home the point.

Booker T. Washington understood this preparation of the spirit when he said: "I do not believe that one should speak unless, deep down in his heart, he feels convinced that he has a message to deliver. When one feels, from the bottom of his feet to the top of his head, that he has something to say that is going to help some individual or some

* Op cit., pp. 70-71.

cause, then let him say it . . . [nothing] can take the place of *soul* in an address."*

Before you deliver a talk, know what there is about it that excites and arouses you. One of America's ablest scientists gave an informative talk on cancer that profoundly stirred a large audience of educated men and women. What happened to the audience, happened to the scientist first.

Getting "Steamed-up"

Many students tell the writer that they have no convictions about which to become animated. If you share their indifference, think of America, for example, as an island in a sea of tyranny, struggling to hold aloft the banner of liberty for free men. Couldn't you get "steamed-up" over the following facts? Couldn't you weave them into a talk that would inspire a sense of responsibility?

In 1948, forty-nine voters in every hundred did not vote.

Thirty-seven automobile dealers in every hundred did not vote.

Thirty-seven independent grocers in every hundred did not vote.

Thirty-three clergymen in every hundred did not vote.

Twenty-five out of every hundred members of Chambers of Commerce did not vote.†

Do these people have something at stake?

Do you?

---

* *Up from Slavery*, p. 176. Doubleday, Doran and Co. (Pocketbook Edition), New York. 1940.

† Herman W. Steinkraus, "The Job of Selling America to the Americans," in *Vital Speeches*, Volume XVI, Number 13.

Did the founding fathers overestimate your zeal for freedom? George S. Counts, noted sociologist, thinks they may have: "As we look back today, we can see that the early champions of democracy viewed the problem too simply. Ordinary men and women seem to be inherently neither good nor bad. Nor do they display much concern about the indefinite perfecting of themselves and institutions. When they have leisure, they seem to prefer enjoying themselves in a thousand non-intellectual and non-political ways. Also, their thirst for knowledge appears to be rather easily satisfied and limited to a fairly narrow range of interests. The men and women of the eighteenth and nineteenth centuries who led the struggle for the emancipation of the masses made the mistake of assuming that the masses of the people were created in their image."*

The "Fine Frenzy" of Ames and Webster

Let's look into our history to see how the early patriots spoke when they wished to move an audience. Fisher Ames addressed the House of Representatives in 1796 on the British Treaty. He depicted the horrors of the border war that would result with the Indians if the treaty were rejected. An old man, a judge in Maine, who heard the burning words of Ames, declared that he felt the "fine frenzy" of the speaker in every line. Ames closed with this climax: "The darkness of midnight will glitter with the blaze of your dwellings. You are a father — the blood of your sons will fatten your cornfield; you are a mother — the war-whoop will wake the sleep of the cradle." The judge

---

* "The End of a Myth About Education and Democracy," in *Vital Speeches,* Volume XV, Number 9.

declared that as he listened to Ames and saw his gestures, the prophecy seemed for a moment a reality: "I shuddered and looked behind me; for I fancied a big Indian with an uplifted tomahawk over me."

A letter by George Ticknor, a Harvard professor and one of America's noted historians, describes his own excitement as he listened to Webster's Plymouth Address. Exclaimed Ticknor: "Three or four times I thought my temples would burst with the gush of blood; for, after all, you must know that I am aware that his address is a collection of wonderful fragments of burning eloquence, *to which his manner gave tenfold*. When I came out, I was almost afraid to come near him. It seemed to me that he was like the mount that might not be touched, and that burned with fire."*

Dead Men Tell No Tales!

There were these — and many others. But what about you? It was not beneath the dignity of great men to unbend in order to drive their ideas to the hearts of their listeners. Whether the message be great or modest, the method of making it interesting and alive remains basically the same. With these speakers, there was no unmotivated yelling or shouting, no affected dramatics or theatricals. There was,

* Material on Ames and Webster from William Matthews, *Oratory and Orators*, pp. 18-20. S. C. Griggs and Co., Chicago. 1878.

however, responsiveness to the meaning and significance of what they wanted to say. And that's the test for you.

As a speaker, is your articulation blurred and sluggish? Is your vocal expression monotonous and flat? Is your face unresponsive and stolid? Is your personality tame and insipid? If you suffer from any of these troubles, they may be only the symptoms of a lack of conviction and enthusiasm.

As Professor William P. Sandford has pointed out: "A speech is ideas, facts, and feelings *in action*. How can you activate others if you yourself are stiff, inhibited, stodgy ?

"Don't be afraid of overdoing action. Nine out of ten persons, by actual count over a twenty-five-year period, need to increase the degree of physical activity that they use in speaking. Of course, you don't want to be a soapbox ranter, but don't go to the other extreme. *Dead men tell no tales!*"*

---

* *Speak Well — and Win!* p. 40. McGraw-Hill Book Co., New York. 1944. Reprinted by permission.

CHAPTER XVII

THE LANGUAGE OF ACTION

Physical Utterance

WE TALK two languages: one for the ear and one for the eye. Ideas can be conveyed in either, but their force is heightened when both languages speak together. This chapter is designed to tell you how to develop skill in using the language of the eye, which is gesture. The point of view expressed by Professor Schubert will be helpful as an introduction to technique: "When you gesture, do it clearly and definitely. Don't fumble and flutter. Get your elbows away from your side and make your gestures sharp and distinct and big enough to be seen by everyone. People can mumble with their hands as well as with their voices. Gestures, like words, can be poorly enunciated. Let your gestures speak up loudly and clearly.

"Also, remember that the larger the audience the bigger and broader your gestures must be. A flip of the hand which carries the idea of indifference to a small group of listeners must become a wave of the arm in a large auditorium. Project your gestures as you project your voice . . . *think* what you're saying; *believe* in what you're saying; and *use your hands whenever you feel the urge to.*"*

Bodily action is not to be regarded merely as posture and gestures of the hands. It includes all the speaker's positions and movements on the platform, including "eye contact," subtle facial shadings and expressions that reveal personal traits, character, and moods; and, in fact, everything the listener sees in the speaker.

---

* Leland Schubert, *A Guide for Oral Communication,* pp. 69-70. Prentice-Hall, Inc., New York. 1948. Reprinted by permission.

To become expressive with the language of action, it is recommended that you apply the principles outlined in this chapter.

Speak Refreshed

To achieve a communicative manner, you must maintain a pleasant attitude of mind and a vibrant tonus of the body. If you are tired and appear before an audience with drooping posture, sagging face, and listless, flabby movements, you can find your condition mirrored in the audience. If you are rested, your muscles respond quickly and meaningfully to your thoughts and feelings. Free from fatigue, you can be a speaker who "is a fountain; one who flows over at the eye and at the lip."

Walk Uprightly

The first and last impressions you make as a speaker are obtained by the audience from the way you walk to and from the platform. You should not shuffle, stride, swagger, tiptoe, plod, or rush. Your walk should be brisk and purposeful, with head up, shoulders high, and arms swinging easily at your side. Your manner should bespeak composure and confidence. Before you speak, look the audience over and assume a comfortable stance. Pause after you finish speaking so that your final words may sink in. Then return to your seat with a firm step.

Appear Alert

Position is no less important to the speaker than to the golfer, batter, tennis player, or dancer. It is the foundation for all physical activities. Posture is the speaker's working base and tells the listeners whether or not he is comfortable, alert, and eager to communicate.

The speaker must not stand fixed throughout his speech. Variety is essential to holding attention. The posture, then, must permit the speaker to shift his weight easily from one foot to the other, either forward or back, or from side to side.

The writer has found that being alert depends not so much upon the position of the feet as upon the distribution of weight. The torso should be kept well forward over the balls of the feet. The weight should be placed on one foot at a time. This will turn the body slightly to one side and counteract the tendency to stand with feet parallel, like sleigh runners. It will check your inclination either to teeter up and down or stand rooted into the platform like a private at attention before a five-star general.

To secure a good posture, practice this exercise: take a big step forward; place the weight completely on the forward foot; then bring the other foot into place at a comfortable angle. One foot will be in advance of the other, and the weight will be on only one foot at a time, permitting easy movement of the relaxed foot to right or left and an unobstrusive pivoting to shift the weight from one foot to the other for a change of position. This brings the body weight over the advanced foot and is the most communicative of all positions. The weight may also be shifted to the foot that is back when there is a slackening in the force of the speech.

The writer has observed that a student will increase the amount of his over-all gesture by twenty to forty percent when his posture is alert, permitting him, if he were to pass out, to fall on his face instead of on the back of his head.

Use your Whole Body

The idea of using the whole body in speech delivery is summed up by Richard C. Borden: "When a good baseball pitcher delivers a ball, he does not deliver with his fingers alone.

"He delivers with his arm, his shoulders, the muscles of his abdomen, his legs — and his brain.

"The good speaker does not deliver with his voice alone.

"He delivers with his body, his hands, his face, his eyes, his emotions, his intellect.

"*Deliver with the full resources of your personality.*

"*Deliver both to your listener's ears—and to his eyes!*"*

---

* *Public Speaking — As Listeners Like It!* p. 90. Harper and Brothers, New York. 1935. Reprinted by permission.

Robert M. La Follette, Sr., distinguished political leader and speaker, is said to have exemplified speaking with the whole body. He was described as "a dynamo of physical energy. . . ." He had "a poised body in which 'every muscle . . . is like a spring of steel' and a speaking countenance capable of the most varied and intense expression."

He spoke with "his head slightly lowered, his shock of brown hair overtopping the face and the right arm extended, the index finger pointing apparently at the very object of his attack. There is a certain fine frenzy in the man . . . . Again he will refer to the noble men that have made history in this country in past years as a heritage of which Americans should be proud, and with clenched fists and uplifted arms, he seems to hold that precious heritage aloft and, gazing at it with open mouth and upturned eyes, invite his hearers to see in substance the very thing his fancy has painted . . . ."[*] It is not advisable, of course, to imitate La Follette or any other speaker. You should develop your own action for making your convictions vivid.

Coordinate your Movements

To gesture with a minimum of energy and a maximum of efficiency, eliminate unnecessary, random, and repeated patterns of movement which call attention to themselves.[†] To be effective, your gestures must be smooth and clear-cut and fit the word to be stressed in the thought unit. The

---

[*] William Norwood Brigance, editor, A *History and Criticism of American Public Address*, II, 962-63. McGraw-Hill Book Co., Inc., New York. 1943. Reprinted by permission. See also Milwaukee *Journal*, Oct. 2, 1897.

[†] See Chapters III and IV for discussion of "Conversational Style" and random movement, pages 42-44.

downstroke of the hand must be executed precisely as the word is spoken, not even a split second before or after.

Timing the action involves the *approach* in which the upstroke of the hand precedes the word to be emphasized. The *stroke* occurs exactly as the word is spoken and is always followed by a *rebound*. The stroke alone carries meaning. Then comes an unconscious relaxation of the gesture as the hand drops to the side after the word has been spoken. This is the *return*.

You may be able to achieve some skill in the *coordination* and *timing* of gesture and arrive at some degree of freedom by practicing the following exercises. Begin by raising the hand on the count of one.

1 - 2 - 3 - 4   5 - 6   7 -

Raise the hand — stroke and rebound — relax the

- 8

hand to side.

Try this:

1 - 2 - 3 - 4   5 - 6   7 - 8
"I   *love*   my country!"

1 - 2 - 3 - 4   5 - 6   7 - 8
"*This*   is the place!"

After the stroke and rebound the arm should come to rest at the side. But where another gesture is to follow immediately, the usual cycle is interrupted, and instead of the *return*, the *stroke* and *rebound* repeat themselves.

For example:

1 - 2 - 3 - 4   5 - 6   7 - 8
Preparation and approach   stroke and rebound   stroke and rebound
"Give   me   *life*,   *liberty*,   and

9 - 10   11 - 12
stroke and rebound   return hand to side.
happiness."

The arm will remain where it is after the stroke on
life, and from that point will execute the two next strokes
on *liberty* and *happiness.* When the series is complete, the
arm drops lightly to the side in a relaxed position.

Shape Gestures to Specific Meanings

To become really proficient as a speaker, you should
adapt your gestures to different types of meaning:

1. *To locate:* point finger or hands at an imaginary object such as a house, a desk, a field, a flock of geese
   on the horizon, a picture, or a mountain.

2. *To picture:* move hands and arms in descriptive
   patterns showing a shape or movement such as the
   curve in the road, the growing of a child, the width
   of a house, the slope of a hill, the features of the
   landscape, or the action in the story.

3. *To emphasize:* clench the fist,
   shake the head, or point the
   finger when you declare how
   much you *love* your country,
   or *need* the funds, or *detest*
   the scheme.

4. *To punctuate:* after the words are spoken, toss the
   head, shrug the shoulders, drop the gaze, raise the
   eyebrows, step forward or back, or use some other
   movement to occupy time for the sake of transition
   or emphasis of an exclamation made or a question
   asked. Such movement would follow these typical
   expressions:

"That's what you think!"

"How could this happen?"

"I told you so!"

"What action shall we take next?"

Speak with your Hands

This is a good place to answer the question: What shall I do with my hands? Eisenson says: "Hand gestures are generally more conventionalized than gestures involving the body as a whole. Examples of these include an open-hand, *palm-up* gesture to signify *agreement* or acceptance of an idea. It may also mean friendship or willingness to join in a friendly relationship. A *palm-down* gesture, on the other hand, signifies *negation*. More emphatic negation than the palm down is the *thumb-down* hand movement. The *pointed index finger* is used to help point out an object or to single out an idea. *Strong feeling* and unity of purpose are revealed through the *clenched fist*."*

When the hands are not gesturing, they may rest in the pockets occasionally. When they do, thrust them all the way in. Don't let a wriggling thumb hanging over the edge of a pocket act as a puppet show to detract attention from your talk. The very best place for the hands is at the side in a still and relaxed manner. This position has proved to be the least conspicuous in studies made by dramatic schools.

To speak fluently with your hands, apply the following seven basic principles, so graphically set forth by Richard

---

* Jon Eisenson, *Basic Speech*, p. 58. The Macmillan Company, New York. 1950. Reprinted by permission.

C. Borden. First of all, he cautions, "Gesture! — Don't gesticulate," and continues:

1. *Start your gestures from the shoulder.*

    Listeners dislike the awkward angularity of elbow gestures.

2. *Lift your gestures well above sea-level* [see-level].

    Listeners dislike "fish" gestures that flop around in the neighborhood of the speaker's knees. [Get them free and away from the body.]

    A gesture well up above waist level fuses with the rest of the speaker's personality.

3. *Start the upstroke of your gesture well in advance of the word selected for emphasis.*

    Listeners dislike startling gestures that dart out abruptly at the last moment.

4. *Make the downstroke of your gesture "click" cleanly on a selected syllable.*

    Listeners like crisp gestures that climax accurately. They dislike groping, weak, uncertain gestures that move around vaguely, reach no particular climax, then fade fuzzily away.

5. *As soon as your gesture "clicks," drop your arm to your side* — without an aftermath of flourish or hand-swinging.

6. *Gesture with "live fingers."*

    Hold an imaginary pineapple in your hand when you gesture. Listeners dislike the unexpressiveness of limp, weakly-closed fingers.

7. *Gesture with discrimination.*

Beware of the temptation merely to beat time with your hands, awarding a gesture to every other word as a matter of routine.

Listeners dislike speakers who hit thought thumb-tacks with gesture sledge hammers.*

CAUTION: Avoid overuse of any one gesture!

Use Your Head

"Two gestures of the head are highly conventionalized. A nod means approval; a lateral shake means disapproval.

"Facial expressions, that is, facial gestures, can be used with great effectiveness to reveal degrees of feeling. The speaker may smile with pleasant approval, or sneer in scornful or contemptuous rejection; his eyes may open wide in surprise or wonder, or half close in anger or hate; he may knit his brows to show concern or concentration, or smooth his brows to reveal relaxation.

"We see that gestures, like many words, may have more than one meaning."†

Don't be a "poker face." Improve the flexibility of your facial muscles by laughing, frowning, smiling, questioning, and scowling before a mirror.

Lincoln in Action

What animation, action, and gesture will do for the speaker may be illustrated in Lincoln. After hearing him for the first time, Joshua Speed said: "I was then fresh from

---

* Borden, *op. cit.*, pp. 99-101.
† Eisenson, *op. cit.*, pp. 58-59.

Kentucky, and had heard many of her great orators. It seemed to me, then, as it seems to me now, that I never heard a more effective speaker. He carried the crowd with him and swayed them as he pleased."*

But Lincoln did not become a speaker of power until "he warmed up to his subject," and this is true of most speakers. Only then did his "dull, listless features drop like a mask. His face lighted up as with an inward fire. The eyes began to sparkle, the mouth to smile, the whole countenance was wreathed in animation. His body began to move in unison with his thought. He straightened up; his form expanded; . . . a splendid and imposing figure . . . . To keep in harmony with his growing warmth, his hands relaxed and fell to his side . . . .

"He had, however, certain typical gestures that the audiences were wont to recall with delight. When Lincoln dropped into explanation, he 'frequently caught hold with his left hand, of the lapel of his coat, keeping his thumb upright and leaving his right hand free to gesticulate.' At moments of great intensity his arms swung into action. When he cried out, 'The advocates of the extension of slavery into the new States will soon find themselves squelched!' he 'raised his right arm to the right, bringing his hand down almost to his feet.' This sweeping gesture he used often, 'stooping forward almost to the ground to enforce some point . . . .' At other times, 'to dot the ideas in the minds of his hearers,' he extended the long, bony index finger of his right hand. When he wanted to show thorough detestation of an idea, he would throw both arms upward, with fists clenched in determination. At other

---

* Joshua F. Speed, *Reminiscences of Abraham Lincoln*, p. 17. John P. Marton and Co., Louisville, Kentucky. 1884.

times, '. . . his clenched hand came down as if he were a blacksmith striking on his anvil . . . .' They were jackknife gestures, quick, incisive, unpredictable in their suddenness, accompanied often by a 'quick turn of the body to right and left as he drove home a red-hot rivet of appeal.' Although Horace White claimed that when Lincoln reached the climax of his speech a stranger might say, 'Why, this man . . . is really handsome,' it is doubtful if his action ever became truly graceful."*

Webster in Action

Of Webster, it was said that his "ordinary manner of speaking was that of a plain man . . . . It was strong, hearty, and downright. His gestures were the gestures of enforcing rather than of describing; such gestures as a sturdy New England farmer under the shadow of the White Hills would use in dictating the tillage of his stubborn acres, or in exemplifying moral monitions to his son, by pointing to those mountains; the open palm of the hand, the pointing finger, the vigorous bringing down of the arm, the easy sidewise wave of all; these were pretty much his variety . . . . He seemed in no way bookish in speaking. He had the broad, deep-ringing tone of a son of the soil; a man who loved broad acres, great cattle, tall trees, and true men. A fresh, hearty, neighborly tone runs through his sentences."†

When Webster was attacking the nondescript party headed by Van Buren, he *dramatized* his idea while he was speaking:

---

* Brigance, *op. cit.*, II, 847-48.
† *Ibid.*, 675.

" 'Why, gentlemen,' said Webster to a gathering of sturdy and hard-featured people, 'that Buffalo Platform is so rickety it will hardly bear the fox-like tread of Mr. Van  Buren'; and as he said 'fox-like tread,' he held out the palm of his left hand, and, with the other hand, played his fingers along his extended arm down to the hand, with a soft running motion, as if to represent the kitten-like advance of the foxy candidate upon his rickety 'platform.' "*

Beecher in Action

The meaning of *dramatization* is further illustrated in this passage about Beecher: "No description of Beecher on the platform would be complete that did not mention his ability to pantomime [i.e. to dramatize]. Beecher *was not content to tell; he wanted to show.* Shenstone gives an amusing example of Beecher's cleverness at mimicry. Henry Ward was speaking of his father Lyman playing his violin:

" 'One day he was amusing himself on his favorite instrument and struck up a genuine jig, which, unsanctified, had been running in his head ever since he was a boy.

" 'Just at that moment the mother came in, and, catching the inspiration of the tune, placed her hands on her hips and actually danced a minuet.

" 'Mr. Beecher described the scene. He stepped back on the platform, placed his hands on his hips, and showed

---

* *Ibid.*, 691.

the audience how his mother did it. He described the consternation of the children. He clasped his hands, rolled up the whites of his eyes like a regular maw-worm, opened his mouth, drew down his lips, and stood the personification of rustic horror.

" 'The whole scene was irresistibly comic.' "*

Start Now

Gestures can be as inconspicuous as a well-chosen necktie or as obvious as a loud one—depending on whether they are spontaneous and impulsive or self-conscious and artificial.

Of gestures, and how to develop them, Lew Sarett and William T. Foster, educators, write: "A speaker should not use too many gestures. In early practice, however, the rule should be ignored, along with all other rules about gesturing. A beginner cannot use too many gestures. The more abundant they are, the more certainly they affect him as a person, the more quickly he breaks down the rigidity of his body and emotional restraints which interfere with self-expression, and the more quickly he develops dynamic speaking. The beginning student may well use a ridiculous number of gestures — ridiculous, that is, to an audience. The speaker uses them not because of what an audience may say about them or think about them, but because of what those gestures may do for him. There will be time enough later on to think about the effect of his gestures on an audience. Then he can easily reduce the number and improve the quality. It is much easier to polish gestures

---

* Brigance, *op. cit.*, I, 279-280.
† *Basic Principles of Speech*, pp. 152-53. Houghton Mifflin Company. Boston. 1946. Reprinted by permission.

than it is to free and develop the impulse to make them."†

The beginner should practice all kinds and types of gestures. He needs to rehearse his talk prior to its delivery in order to stir within himself a strong feeling about the ideas he wishes to express. When he faces his audience, he should throw himself into his speech and forget about gesturing. If this advice is followed, correct habits will be formed that finally carry over to every speaking situation — provided the speaker is properly motivated to deliver a message.

The writer has seen hundreds of students who have kept determinedly at it, learn to gesture meaningfully. The process is much like learning to play the piano. The speaker, like the pianist, must practice until he has confidence in his ability to execute the physical and mechanical aspects of his art. Spontaneity and forgetfulness of technique ensue.

The advice of Henry Clay, orator on American political problems from 1806-50, is to the point. Clay worked diligently to develop his magnificent power of speech, and later in life, he described his efforts to a class of law students: "I owe my success in life to one single fact—namely, that at an early period I commenced and continued for some years the practice of daily reading and speaking the contents of some historical or scientific book. These off-hand efforts were sometimes made in a cornfield; at others in the forest; and not infrequently in some distant barn, with the horse and ox for my only auditors. It is to this practice of the art of all arts that I am indebted for the primary and leading impulses that stimulated my progress and have shaped and moulded my entire destiny."*

---

* Brigance, *op. cit.*, II, 607.

CHAPTER XVIII

THE VOICE OF DISTINCTION

AN IMPRESSIVE DINNER was given by a literary society in Milwaukee. At the conclusion, Madame Modjeska asked if she might not express her appreciation by giving a short Polish recitation. Otis Skinner, one of the guests, describes what she did: "Her liquid voice became by turns melancholy and gay, impassioned, tragic, light with happiness, and blighting with bitterness. There was not a note in the gamut of emotions she did not touch. She finished with a recurrent rhythm, fateful and portentous. We were clutched by the spell. We didn't know what it was about, but we knew it was something tremendous. Someone asked what it was. She answered with a sly smile, 'I merely recited the alphabet.' "*

Sell with Your Voice

This example is not cited to encourage tricks with the voice, but to highlight the fact that the voice possesses unique power to express feelings and moods and to touch off every human emotion. For this reason it is one of the most important of all factors in speaking and persuasion. A customer told a salesman that his remarkable power in selling was not in his product or in what he said but in his resonant, friendly voice. "Your voice," he said, "should be credited with much of your phenomenal success and is worth hundreds of thousands of dollars to you as a salesman." What is true of salesmen is equally true of speakers generally. If you wish to attain maximum speech power, develop your speaking voice.

---

* Cornelia Otis Skinner, *Family Circle*, pp. 37-38. Houghton Mifflin Co., Boston. 1948.

Voice Begins in the Mind

In reality a good voice begins in the mind. It stems from a desire to communicate something worth while. The voice is not an ornament. In fact, a merely "beautiful" voice is often annoying and distasteful. It may be melodious and sleep-inducing. It may convey no basic interest, convictions, or enthusiasms. On the other hand, a voice of poor quality may be powerful if it speaks vital ideas and sincere feelings. A labor leader in a recent speech pleaded for the development of men "whose voices may not be loud, but whose skillful persuasion can be heard above the misunderstanding in men's hearts."

The voice of Lincoln was high-pitched and nasal, but because of his noble character and deep-seated convictions, it had the intensity to persuade and thrill his audiences. The fact that some good speakers have been handicapped with poor voices should not justify any one of us in tolerating a deficiency in himself that guided practice might remedy.

The fundamental factor in voice production is identical with the essential element in bodily action. More important than gesture or voice is the urge to communicate. The speaker must be brimming over with zeal and be full of interesting facts and illustrations. If he is shy, disinterested, unsure, or dead on his feet, he will not be able to project a vigorous tone. If he is frightened or self-conscious, he may tighten and hold rigid the muscles of breathing. The vast majority of speakers who cannot project their voices are unable to do so because they *think* they can't. *Timid, indifferent individuals are rarely able to hold an audience.*

If the desire to convey a message is sufficiently strong, voice and body will, in most cases, respond meaningfully. Training on some of the fine points is all that may be necessary.

Be Your Own Critic

Become conscious of your own voice. Learn to listen to it. To hear it as others do, get an *ear-view* of the sounds that come from your vocal instrument. Only then will you be able to discover and correct its defects.

Record your voice! This method provides the best way to hear yourself as others hear you. Commercial and home recording facilities exist nearly everywhere today. Using such a recording as a "photograph" of your voice will enable you to detect peculiarities in tone quality, pitch level, and inflection, as well as in phrasing and in use of pauses. It will  help you adjust the rate, pitch, and volume. It will also assist you with a related problem. You will be able to discover bad pronunciations, slovenliness, and indistinctness in your articulation. An occasional recording of a talk you are making will help you eliminate mistakes in grammar and sentence structure. Get the help of a teacher of speech if you need professional advice. Remember: Do not let the discovery that you have some inadequacies destroy your confidence or morale. Work on your specific difficulties in private practice. Every speaker has some problems to solve.

Improve Your Voice

The mere exercise of your voice will not greatly improve its effectiveness. You must discover where it is deficient before plotting a course of action. To achieve a voice that will be dynamic and persuasive, measure its qualities according to a standard such as the following by Professor Anderson. (Suggestions by the writer are included for improving each aspect of voice production.)

"1. *Adequate loudness.* Nothing is more distressing than the attempt to hear what a speaker is saying when all that reaches one's ear is a low, weak murmur out of which an intelligible phrase arises now and then . . . . If people frequently have to ask you to repeat what you have said, take warning and determine whether your voice possesses adequate loudness."

If you have trouble in being heard, practice speaking to the person who sits on the back row. Talk as if you were throwing the tones out in front of you. Try this on: "Hello, hello, hello; one, one, one; tip of the tongue, tip of the tongue, tip of the tongue." Practice speaking, not shouting, above the noise of the radio turned on a full blast. Have someone turn it off suddenly. This will enable you to determine how forcefully you are projecting your voice.

Caution should be observed, however, in the use of power. Speaking with the throat under muscular strain will destroy a good voice. Being heard does not so much depend upon loudness as upon resonance, accurate articulation, and controlled modulation. Professor Anderson says: "Tone production requires but little effort in the throat. While it is true, of course, that tone is really initiated in the larynx, the student of voice will be greatly aided if he thinks of the effort involved as coming from the middle of the body, the place where the breathing activity is centered. After all, the breath does furnish the motive power of voice; tone is supported and sustained by and from the breathing muscles, and the throat should be regarded as a more passive agent where tone is megaphoned, molded, and built up. This concept is particularly helpful in the development of volume and projection of tone without the high pitch and evidences of strain which often accompany increase in volume."*

"2. *Clearness and purity of tone.* Is your voice clear and bell-like or could it be called 'fuzzy,' hoarse, breathy, husky, nasal, or throaty? The good voice must be free from disturbing, unpleasant elements in the tone." Most of these difficulties are clinical problems. Remedies should be applied under the direction of a qualified speech pathologist.

"3. *A pleasing and effective pitch level* . . . . Individuals differ somewhat in their best pitch level, but for every voice there will be found a key at which it performs most effectively and pleasantly." To find the best pitch level for your voice, go to a piano and sing "ah" down to your lowest comfortable pitch. Then go up four whole steps. This should be very close to your best speaking pitch.

"4. *Ease and flexibility.* The normal voice is responsive and is characterized by a degree of variety and melody . . . and should not convey the impression of being forced or

* Virgil A. Anderson, *Training the Speaking Voice*, pp. 58-59. Oxford University Press, New York. 1942. Reprinted by permission.

labored." Lack of excessive tension in the throat muscles, coupled with adequate control of the breath supply, will produce a pleasing voice quality, if there are no abnormal conditions in your throat, nose, and mouth. To improve your control of breath for speaking, pant like a dog, expel the breath slowly with a prolonged hum, count with increasing force from one to ten. Practice relaxation by letting your head hang limp, massaging the muscles of your throat and jaws, yawning, and singing the vowel tones softly.

NOTE: Any program of exercises that is set up must be followed *regularly* and *intelligently* if any good is to result.

"5. A *vibrant, sympathetic quality* . . . . a voice possessing this quality can be said to have warmth and resonance; it is *alive.* " If the voice is to be alive, *you* must be alive. Emotion puts range, color, and richness into the voice.

"6. *Clearness and ease of diction.* The good voice is easily intelligible without being conspicuously so. The speaker is readily understood because his diction is clear and distinct; he doesn't mutilate his speech by omitting or swallowing sounds and syllables."*

A troubled wife came to her physician to get some advice about her husband. She was disturbed because he talked in his sleep. The doctor assured her that he could easily be cured. The wife hesitated and replied, "Well, that's not exactly what I want. I'd like you to give him something to make him speak more distinctly."

Three faults interfere with clearness of diction: (1) immovable jaw; (2) idle tongue; (3) lazy lips. To improve the character of your speaking, read aloud regularly every

---

* Anderson, *op. cit.*, pp. 8-9.

day. Practice tongue twisters rapidly and precisely. Articulate vigorously the consonant sounds during your practice.

Titillating Tongue Teasers

Here's a twenty-second test often given to candidates for radio announcing. If you can read it aloud without mistakes in that time, you're *good*:

"I bought a batch of baking powder and baked a batch of biscuits. I brought a big basket of biscuits back to the bakery and baked a basket of big biscuits. Then I took the big basket of biscuits and the basket of big biscuits and mixed the big biscuits with the basket of biscuits that was next to the big basket and put a bunch of biscuits from the basket into the box. Then I took the box of mixed biscuits, a biscuit mixer, biscuit basket, and brought the basket of biscuits and the box of mixed biscuits and the biscuit mixer to the bakery and opened a can of sardines."

Try these:

1. He sawed six long, slim, sleek, slender saplings.

2. "Are you copper-bottoming them, my man?" "No, I'm aluminuming 'em, mum."

3. Amidst the mists and coldest frosts,
   With stoutest wrists and loudest boasts,
   He hits his fists against the posts
   And still insists he sees the ghosts.

4. A skunk sat on a stump;
   The skunk thought that the stump stunk;
   And the stump thought that the skunk stunk.

Exaggerate the lip movement in speaking the following sentences:

1. Peter Piper picked a peck of pickled peppers.
2. Bubble, bubble boiled the pot.
3. The wire was wound round the wheel.

Move the jaw in a rotary movement and then repeat: "ouch" a number of times.

No Growls — Tune Your Vowels

The musical quality of your speech depends upon openness of vowels and vowel combinations (diphthongs). The vowel is the heart of the word and provides the resonance. Enunciate it roundly and accurately. Take the simple line, "Oh, I'm lonely and weary, and I hope to go home." Smother the vowel sounds by speaking in a staccato manner. Then enunciate them with complete freedom and fulness of expression. Notice the warmth of the voice quality you put into "lonely," "weary," and "hope." Read aloud poetic selections written in a sublime or reverential mood, such as the Biblical Psalms or the "Recessional" of Kipling. Try, also, selections such as the following:

> Gold, gold, gold, gold.
> Bright and yellow, hard and cold,
> Molten, graven, hammered, rolled,
> Heavy to get, and light to hold,
> Hoarded, bartered, bought and sold,
> Stolen, borrowed, squandered, doled,
> Spurned by the young, and hugged by the old,
> To the very verge of the churchyard mould.

Caution

Carelessness and too much speed are usually responsible for such distortions as:

"Mr. Pre'dent, Ladies 'n Gen'lmen: The subjec' of my 'dress is manafacturin' an' perduction in Ioway."

Such vulgar phrases as the following are common:

"Where 'dja go?" "Watyadoon?"

"Iwannago." "Ah'll be seenya."

"I'll meetcha!" "Howjaddo."

"Didja like th' movin' pitcher?"

The typical speaker possesses few actual defects in his speech. His real problems nearly all stem from carelessness. Especially is he apt to be slovenly with his pronunciation. One needs to be precise when speaking the following words and others like them:

while (not wile) film (not fillum)

get (not git) history (not histry)

for (not fer) general (not genral)

because (not bekuz) family (not famly)

just (not jist) biographical (not bigraphical)

any (not iny) creek (not crick)

such (not sich) build (not buil')

city (not cidy) fifth (not fif')

battle (not baddle) guest (not gues')

government (not gov'munt) almost (not awmost)

eleven (not 'leven) already (not awready)

hundred (not hunderd) picture (not pitcher)

partner (not pardner) beautiful (not beaudiful)

athletics (not athaletics) vegetable (not vegtable)

It is a common practice for speakers to drop the g in words ending in ing, giving the speech a sloppy effect. Avoid goin'; say going.

Vary the Pitch

The monotonous voice is not necessarily on a dead level. It may result from a fixed or set pattern in the use of pitch, rate, and volume, and may tire the listener because of its deadly repetition. Its pattern is not so much a "one-tone" voice as a "one-tune" voice. To overcome monotony in pitch, practice inflections in statements such as the following:

"Oh, do you think you know?"

"Why, certainly I'm going to the football game."

"Oh, I'm weary, discouraged, and yearn to go home."

"Oh, yeah, that's what you think!"

For further practice, imagine yourself before an audience that you wish to arouse in behalf of the abolition of slavery. Speak these words of William Lloyd Garrison in an impassioned manner:

"I am aware that many object to the severity of my language; but is there not cause for severity? I will be as harsh as Truth and as uncompromising as Justice. On this subject I do not wish to think, or speak, or write with moderation. No! No! Tell a man whose house is on fire to give a moderate alarm; tell him to moderately rescue his wife from the hands of the ravisher; tell the mother to gradually extricate her babe from the fire into which it has fallen — but urge me not to use moderation in a cause like the present. I am in earnest — I will not equivocate — I will not excuse — I will not retreat a single inch — and I will be heard."

If you want to be forceful, control the pitch of your voice. Without contrast, everything you speak will sound unimportant.

Vary the Rate

The most suitable rate of utterance is between 145 to 165 words a minute. Fewer than one hundred words a minute is too slow even for weighty materials. The writer hears many more complaints about the speaker who talks too slowly than the one who talks too fast, although talking too fast is a far more common fault. It is a severe handicap to stall and plod and speak at a measured, laborious, and jerky pace. Unless you have unusual distinctness of utterance and facility of inflection, you should seldom speak faster than one hundred fifty words a minute.

Ordinary thought is neither quick nor slow. But the sublime, grand, solemn, tired, and depressed tend to slow down the movement of ideas. On the other hand the gay, eager, impetuous, and exciting, speed up expression.

The rate may be varied by prolonging the vowels according to the particular quality of the idea the word expresses. The umpire calls: "S-t-r-i-i-k-e O-o-n-e!"

Develop a feeling for the "idea-sounds" of words. Many words sound the way they mean. You *slip* on a banana peel, but you *slide* home. You *knock* on a door, but you *jump* the creek. You listen to the *crack* of the thunder, but you hear the *braying* of the donkey. The fly *flits*, but the wild duck *flies*, the bird *chirps*, the cow *moos*.

Silence Is Golden

An excellent way to achieve variety in speaking is to pause at the right times. The ears of the listener are not as quick as his eyes, and meaningful silence is required to permit the thought to sink in.

Most beginning speakers fear silence, not realizing that it is as necessary to intelligent speaking as sound. The speaker must taste the flavor of the words in his mouth as he utters them. He must not hurl them carelessly into space. Pausing enables the speaker to convey subtleties of meaning. Observe how the comedian or practiced speaker can "squeeze a laugh" or raise a lump in the throat through skillful timing. The speaker helps his audience get his meaning by expressing his ideas in thought units punctuated by pauses.

Vary the Force

A speaker must be heard, but if monotony is to be avoided, he must be heard in varying degrees and forms of force. This contrast in the stress and volume enables him to show the relative importance of ideas. In the sentence, "I like red apples," there are but four words. When the force is applied differently to each word, the meaning changes. With no stress on any of the words, it is a plain statement.

"*I* like red apples," emphasizes that I'm the one who prefers red apples.

"I *like* red apples," says how much I relish them.

"I like *red* apples," highlights the kind I enjoy most.

"I like red *apples*," suggests that any kind of apples will please me.

Force may be applied vigorously as in the explosive forms or gently as in the effusive forms. It is varied by increasing or decreasing the loudness of a word or phrase. Change the force constantly for greatest emphasis. A good speaker may change his force by dropping his volume to a whisper that is arresting in its contrast to previous delivery. There is a tendency to raise the pitch through tension whenever the force is increased. The speaker should be careful to keep his voice at the most pleasant and desirable pitch level.

Ascend the Ladder

The word *climax* describes the high point of a speech. It derives from a Greek word which literally means *ladder*. To be interesting, a speech must climb progressively toward a climax. The thoughts should be arranged in the order of increasing importance, and the delivery should be intensified in all its aspects as the speaker approaches the end of his talk. Material, choice of language, and composition all combine to achieve a climax, but the effect of the climax largely depends upon delivery.

The pattern for the *build up* of the speech to its natural conclusion is prescribed by a country lawyer:

> Begin low,
> Advance slow,
> Rise higher,
> Strike fire,
> Then retire.

CHAPTER XIX

HUMAN RELATIONS IN SPEAKING

"When Jesus finished his speech, the crowds were astounded at his teaching; for he taught them like an authority, not like their own scribes."* And about his speaking in the temple Mark records: "Now the mass of the people listened with delight to him."† There was a strength in the personal nature of Jesus that was convincing and eloquent. As a power in effective speaking, this soundness of mind and spirit has no equal. In the case of Jesus, it far surpassed, in its force and appeal, the flawless erudition and superior learning of the Scribes and Pharisees. The appeal of sincerity so evident when Jesus spoke remains unequalled in our own time.

The Ethics of Winning Friends

Speaking is an intensely personal expression of the man who speaks. What he is as a person on the platform cannot be separated successfully from what he is off the platform. Any attempt at such a division of self to effect a platform personality inconsistent with one's basic character is futile. The speaker may delude himself and some listeners for a time, but ultimately the audience sees through his sham. Just as an institution is measured by the lengthened shadow of a man, so is the worth of a speech measured by the integrity of the speaker himself. In the remaining pages of this book are presented the qualities of personality and character requisite to the ideal speaker.

---

* Reference is here made to the Sermon on the Mount. See Moffatt translation of the Bible, Matthew 7: 28-29.

† *Ibid.*, Mark 12: 37.

Second only to health, the desire to be liked by others and to get along well with people are the chief unfulfilled ambitions of adult Americans. The University of Chicago and the American Association for Adult Education spent $25,000 in a two-year study which determined these facts.

It is a common observation that the person who is well-liked has little difficulty in gaining acceptance for his ideas. One finds it almost impossible to refuse a friend. We often hear it said, "*You* ask him; he's *your* friend. He'll do it for *you*." This may be a proper use of friendship in many cases, but when used as a device of chicanery, it becomes a practice to be condemned. It degrades human relations. "William J. Fallon, the Great Mouthpiece, successfully defended 127 murderers; no jury ever returned a death verdict against any of his clients. A rival once asked him: 'How do you win so many acquittals?' Fallon replied, 'Most lawyers try to make the jury favorable to their client. The thing to do is to make them favorable to you yourself. After that, it's as easy as shooting fish in a barrel.' "*

The speaker *does* need skill in winning friends to himself and his cause. But he has the moral responsibility of considering whether or not his listeners are mere "fish in a barrel" to be preyed upon by his clever artifices or human beings whose personal integrity is to be respected and esteemed. Justice Cardozo of the United States Supreme Court said: "It is strange how many lawyers come before us who have it in their minds that they can outsmart the Supreme Court. This thought is so evident by their actions and their pleas that all of us seem to sense it at once. We

* Henry Morton Robinson, "How Lawyers Have Won Cases," in *Reader's Digest*, July 1941, p. 91. Reprinted by permission.

merely exchange smiles and let the wrong-thought holder defeat himself."

Don't Be Misled

If you study popular writings in human relations, you will find a variety of recipes contrived to enable people to win the approval of others. Among them, you will sense a widespread tendency to overpopularize superficial personality traits. Take caution! These are of slight importance unless the basic qualities of character are present in the individual. The extensive studies of Dr. M. E. Bonney, psychologist, have brought this principle into sharp focus: "One of the fallacies of the self-improvement books is that they make winning friends a matter of developing a few social gestures or techniques, to the neglect of the *total individual*. I have found in my studies that a person is well-accepted more because of what he is and does in the way of making a contribution to the group, than because of one or more of the traits usually considered necessary for the winning of friends.

"Even if you have a moderate number of obnoxious traits, such as being bossy or untidy, you may yet be the most popular member of your group if you have strong, aggressive traits which contribute to *group success*. Popularity is not the superficial thing it is often assumed to be, but is tied up with the most basic traits of personality and character. Winning friends and achieving popularity is the end result of a good general development, the achievement of many kinds of competence and preparation for all the problems of life."

Let us ponder Dr. Bonney's concluding words: "Winning friends is not nearly as easy as many writers would have us believe, but is, instead, the consequence of a *good general development of personality and character*, and a sound preparation for meeting adequately the problems of life. In other words, you must *do something* and *be something*, if you want to be popular, win friends, and be a happy, well-adjusted, and influential human being."*

Personality Is Your Mirror

Dr. Bonney's research shows clearly that there are two clusters of traits possessed by the individual and that neither by itself is sufficient to produce a leader of significance and appeal. One cluster of traits molds the *good* man. It is called *character* and is discussed in the final chapter of this book. The second determines the manner in which the individual expresses his character or inner self to others; it is the way in which he *shows* himself to the world and is called his *personality*. The rest of this chapter is designed to help you improve this part of your personal equipment.

An attractive personality *can* be developed; it is yours for the making! Dr. Henry C. Link explains that you pos-

---

* Quoted by Albert Edward Wiggam, in *New Techniques of Happiness*, pp. 107-09. Wilfred Funk, Inc., New York, 1948. Reprinted by permission.

sess personality to the degree that you have "*developed* habits which interest and serve other people." Your personality is not measured in terms of how much property you own nor on the basis of your listing in the social register. More accurately it is appraised in the light of what you do when you are with other people. Personality is not a possession but an activity. It grows as a result of an investment of vitality—physical, mental, emotional, and spiritual.

The first test of a leader is: "Can I put the common good above my own selfish interests?" The gist of the matter is that you become what you are by reason of your *habit patterns*. If you are kind, it is only because you have acquired the habit of thinking kindly of other people. If you are thorough, it is only because you have developed the habit of taking care of each detail. If you are good-natured, it is only because you have secured the habit of restraining your aggressive impulses under trying circumstances. The number of such habits is almost endless. Note how closely they are interwoven with character traits. Let us examine the desirable personality traits as they are listed and defined by Joy Elmer Morgan, noted educator:

1. *Flexibility* — The ability to change and grow, to listen, to question, to fit in with the plans of others.

2. *Cheerfulness* — The habit of enjoying life and of expecting the best [of minimizing annoyances and dealing with others in a spirit of patience, charitableness, and good humor].

3. *Poise* — The ability to keep serene amid trying circumstances.

4. *Loyalty* — The habit of being faithful to friendships and responsibilities.

5. *Enthusiasm* — Capacity for believing in the success of worth-while things.

6. *Initiative* — The power to think out things to do and to go forward.

7. *Dependability* — The habit of being on time and of keeping engagements.

8. *Industry* — The habit of staying at tasks until properly finished.

9. *Courage* — The moral stamina to stand firmly for right, truth, and justice.

10. *Good judgment* — The ability to consider evidence, to weigh carefully and tolerantly; to decide wisely.*

One hundred outstanding men in business named the following ten qualities as the most essential characteristics of successful men: Sympathy, address, enthusiasm, sincerity, personal appearance, optimism, scholarship, vitality, fairness, and reserve or dignity.†

Cultivate Pearls of Good Behavior

Energy and vitality may be consumed in acquiring the wrong kinds of habits and personality traits. A survey was made of the employees of nearly one hundred large corporations. It revealed that individuals who were dismissed or retarded were found to have displeasing personalities. They were afflicted with one or more of the following negative traits. They were discourteous, irresponsible, dishonest, dis-

---

* Joy Elmer Morgan, "Your Personality in the Making," *Personal Growth* Leaflet Number Seven, published by The National Education Association, Washington, D. C.

† Contributed by Dr. Adam S. Bennion, distinguished lecturer, educator, and business executive.

loyal, unadaptable, absent, and tardy for trivial reasons; they dressed in poor taste and were smugly satisfied with themselves, showing little or no interest in self-improvement. These negative traits could have been turned to good use if these individuals had been stimulated to build opposite and desirable habits. As Emerson explains, our faults may prick and sting us until we "acquire habits of self-help; and thus, like the wounded oyster, we mend our shell with pearl. Our strength grows out of our weakness." Some declare such a self-improvement program requires too much self-denial and self-sacrifice. They forget that any personality traits we acquire exact a cost.

There is an old Spanish proverb which advises: " 'Take what you want,' says God, 'take it and *pay* for it.' " Whatever kind of personality you have is the kind you pay for. Commenting on this idea, Dr. Harry Emerson Fosdick says: "Consider the lopsidedness of our ordinary thought of self-denial. When we talk about the sacrificial life, it is commonly understood to mean one thing only, the costliness of goodness, the self-sacrifice required in a clean, controlled, high-minded, useful person . . . .

"That, however, is a one-sided view of sacrificial living. Everything we choose, whether good or bad, we pay for. If a man choose debauchery and dissipation, we commonly call it self-indulgence, but think again! Self-indulgence — to live a wasted, dissipated life? Upon the contrary, such living is self-sacrifice, the costliest self-sacrifice a person can make, giving up everything that most renders life worth while, throwing diamonds on the counter to buy dust . . . . Surely George Washington lived a sacrificial life, but so did Benedict Arnold, heaven have mercy on him!"

As stated previously, the principal objection raised to the self-improvement books is the insincerity and hypocrisy that they cultivate in superficial people. But if improvement is to be made in human affairs, there must be a beginning. Shakespeare wrote: "Assume a virtue if you have it not." A virtue may become permanent through repeated assumptions. This practice is exactly what Benjamin Franklin pursued. He declared that he "wished to live without committing any fault at any time." He concentrated on one virtue each week, keeping daily check on the other twelve, and repeated the cycle. His success in attaining one of these, humility, is verified by his own testimony: "This mode, which I at first put on with some violence, became at length so easy, and so habitual to me, that perhaps for these fifty years past no one has ever heard a dogmatical expression escape me."*

Hang the Villain of Misunderstanding

The man of sterling character and pleasing personality may fail as an effective leader unless he can communicate his desirable qualities to others. Inept communication is responsible for much wretchedness in human relations. Professor Mayo, renowned Harvard scholar, after lifelong study, says: "I believe

---

* The virtues Franklin worked so diligently to acquire are: temperance, silence, order, resolution, frugality, sincerity, justice, moderation, cleanliness, tranquility, chastity, humility, and industry. See one of the many editions of his *Autobiography* for a detailed account of his excellent program for self-improvement.

that social study should begin with . . . communication: that is, the capacity of an individual to communicate his feelings and ideas to another, the capacity of groups to communicate effectively and intimately with each other. This problem is, beyond all reasonable doubt, the outstanding defect that civilization is facing today."*

Unless people understand one another, the whole structure of our society collapses. Those who fail to understand remain as strangers. Misunderstanding spawns strife and unhappiness everywhere. It tears husband and wife apart, drives the child to run away from home, robs the worker of the bread he might earn for his family, incites the picket line and the lockout, goads nations to the slaughter of their youth on fields of battle, and prevents the establishment of lasting peace after the carnage. It is the arch villain of our age. The poet truly says:

> Here lies the tragedy of our race;
> Not that men are poor:
> All men know something of poverty;
> Not that men are wicked,
> Who can claim to be good ?
> Not that men are ignorant,
> Who can boast that he is wise ?
> But that men are *strangers*.

Our communication is weak and is responsible for the misunderstanding that everywhere prevails, according to Major Charles T. Estes of the Federal Conciliation and Mediation Service. Our stupid habits create three principal defects in dealing with people: (1) Poor *transmission* or inadequate use of language and speech; (2) poor *reception*

---

* Elton Mayo, *The Social Problems of an Industrial Civilization*, p. 22. Division of Research, Harvard University, Boston. 1945. Reprinted by permission.

or imperfect listening with the mind free from the static of fear, anger, prejudice, or suspicion; (3) poor *assimilation* of what is heard.

Our deficiencies lie in our attitudes and techniques. We are hateful, unpleasant, abrupt, and quarrelsome. We argue, contradict, and make dogmatic assertions. We put people in a rebellious and maddened mood, and they bristle on the defensive. We force an issue from every difference of opinion, and in so doing we close the mind of the other person to what we have to say. Instead, we should ask him questions in order to find an area of agreement, and do it in a friendly and understanding manner.

Speak the Universal Language of Tone

Misunderstanding is initiated, grows, and festers in the habitual misuse of the voice. All quarreling begins and is fanned into violence by raised voices. The person who comes to you for a fight, usually *shouts*. If you do not shout back, there can be no fight. If you control your voice by acquiring the right attitudes and habits, you control the situation. In fact, a controlled voice puts you in command under all circumstances. Don't shout! Learn to speak commandingly without seeming to command.

Hughes Mearns, a contemporary advocate of the creative approach to human relations, reveals to us the unbelievable power of the language of tone. These are his words: "Twenty years of work on problems of human relations have made me aware that one of the prime reasons people fail to get along smoothly with one another is the seemingly unknown fact that the voice tone often *transmits* a message contradictory to the one registered by the words we speak."

The writer believes so sincerely in Professor Mearns' point of view that he is pleased to reprint in these pages a further excerpt:

Know Tone Values

"The commonest misuse of the voice tone is to be noted in polite phrases that may thinly conceal boredom or dislike — as when one gushes insincerely, 'I loved your party, my dear!' or in the rapid-fire breathlessness of, 'It was so darling of you to have us over to meet your charming guest. We adored every minute of it, didn't we, Charles?' . . .

"Other examples of misused voice tone causing friction in human dealings include the voice of illness that lingers on into health and sometimes hangs on forever; the girlish voice prolonged absurdly into middle age; the voice of resigned patience that, to children, is worse than open scoldings. Then there is the cares-of-the-day voice, taking the housework to dinner, bringing the office home at night.

"Complete awareness of the reality of tone language is necessary before much personal improvement can be made. Try translating the words we hear into the true declarations which the tone used reveals as lying back of the words. One 'How do you do!' becomes 'How *nice* you are!' Another 'How do you do!' becomes 'Go to the devil!' A 'Do you expect to be away long?' may turn into 'Here's hoping you *never* come back!' A 'Let's see more of one another' translates into 'Never again if I can help it!'

"After recognition of this common double talk should come deliberate practice in the use of desirable tones. This cannot be put on like gestures or make-up. True feeling lies deep. It takes energy to bring it up and to send forth our best self as the carrier of ordinary words. However, if maintenance of good relations among those we love is important to us, it is worth working for.

Be Sincere

"Sincerity in conventional social matters is best conveyed by a simple lowering of the voice and a calculated slowing up of speech. *Drop the complimentary speech altogether when no decent feeling is back of it.* Fortunately, most of our communications with one another may be carried on in the level tone of literal statement, which suggests no hidden meanings or insinuations . . . . So when someone in the family asks, 'Where is the screw driver?' the answer should call nobody to account for not knowing, convey no annoyance at being asked, express no interest in what the tool is wanted for. It should be a cool and disinterested statement of fact. There is nothing like the deliberate use of this tone to reduce tensions . . . .

Be Friendly

"The next step is to practice the *stranger tone*. In many families guests or even strangers often receive a more friendly voice vibration than is commonly served out to members of the household. Imagine husband, wife, or child as a person met for the first time. For example, the mother might think of her own child as a new little boy just come into the neighborhood. Then the sharp admonitory tone, that has often become habitual, is dropped; friendliness is carried with every spoken word. It is a device that has worked well; you should see the child respond with cheery obedience rather than sullen resistance. The husband hears again, after long years, that friendly voice of interest-in-him, that touch of a laugh in the words, that assuring tone which abolishes past and future cares and lives only in the blessed present . . . .

"The language of tone was in use a million years before man invented artificial words. Good communications can still be made even when language barriers block the way. I have heard friendly white men talk in our language with Indians who reply in theirs; goodwill is expressed and understood without either comprehending the other's speech. Social workers tell me that with immigrants a *smile*, a *gesture*, and *words charged with welcome* and *helpfulness* are all that is needed to banish apprehension and induce trust and friendliness, despite the fact that they can't understand a word that is said.

"Conscious use of the language of tone will enrich all human relationships. So look over your tone language . . . get acquainted with this thing that shouts our secrets to all the world. Remake your conversation; get yourself a new voice. Scare yourself with the great truth that something precious is lost with every failure to express truly your real feeling."*

Forbear Offense

A person may have a vast knowledge of science, mathematics, arts, and letters, and yet remain incapable of cooperating with his fellow men. Benjamin Franklin was not a born diplomat. As a young man he offended and antagonized people when he might have been tactful and persuasive. Here is his account of his awakening: "A Quaker friend

---

* Hughes Mearns, "Tone Up Your Voice — and Personality!" in *Rotarian* and *Reader's Digest*, June 1944, pp. 15-17. Reprinted by permission.

informed me that I was generally thought proud; that my pride showed itself in conversation; that I was not content with being right, but was overbearing and insolent. So I determined to cure myself of this folly and add *humility* to my list of twelve virtues I was working to acquire."

Franklin's *attitude* changed. And here is the key to the acquisition of all the personality traits that are termed pleasing and helpful. A speaker who develops a *constructive attitude* expresses himself with tact, interest, and understanding. How thoroughly Franklin had altered his attitude may be seen in his decision to change his actions. He said: "I made it a rule to forbear all direct contradictions to the sentiments of others, and all positive assertions of my own. I even forbade myself the use of every word or expression in the language that imported fixed opinion, such as *certainly, undoubtedly,* etc., and I adopted instead of them, *I conceive, I apprehend,* or *I imagine* a thing to be so; or *it so appears to me at present.* When another asserted something I thought in error, I denied myself the pleasure of contradicting him abruptly, and of showing immediately some absurdity in his proposition; and in answering I began by observing that in certain cases or circumstances his opinion would be right, but in the present case there *appeared* or *seemed* to me some difference, etc.

"I soon found the advantage in this change in my manner; the conversations I engaged in went on more pleasantly. The modest way in which I proposed my opinions procured them a readier reception and less contradiction; I had less mortification when I was found to be in the wrong, and I more easily prevailed with others to give up their mistakes and join with me when I happened to be in the right."

Charity for All

Franklin has had eminent company in this experience of altering human relations. As a young man, Lincoln formed the habit of writing caustic letters and poems. He dropped them on neighboring doorsteps and along the road where they could easily be found. His ridicule aroused resentment and the desire for revenge. Through bitter experience, Lincoln learned the folly of his ways. Later in life he said: " 'A drop of honey catches more flies than a gallon of gall.' So with men. If you would win a man to your cause, first convince him that you are his sincere friend." Lincoln became a symbol of tolerance and compassion, and he stirred the hearts of men with these immortal words: "With malice toward none, with charity for all."

CHAPTER XX

YOU SPEAK WHAT YOU ARE

YOU CAN LEARN TO SPEAK is more than a title to a treatise on speaking. It expresses a faith in you as a person — you whose inner convictions should be heard in the forum of our democracy. This book might properly have been called *You Must Learn to Speak,* for you *must* develop skill in communication if your voice is to ring out clearly above the confusion of tongues prevailing in today's world.

Prepare for Leadership

Never in world history have we needed more urgently a high quality of leadership. America is plagued by weariness in the pursuit of high purpose. "Many indeed are those who will not face the atomic age — who refuse to accept that *we must be pioneers again.* Greater yet is the number who have the courage but who lack the vision and the leadership — who know the challenge is here but know not how to meet it, and hence try to forget it exists and just plod along in the old pattern, attending to immediate problems and giving no thought to the morrow. The task ahead isn't as simple as enduring physical torture in testimony of religious faith; it isn't as simple as fighting Indians, stalking grizzly bears, and building railroads. Not that these things were easy — but the task ahead is the far harder, the far more complex one of finding truth, fighting ideas with finer ideas, revitalizing democracy — averting Armageddon!"*

---

*Elvis J. Stahr, jr., "The Challenge of the Critical Century," in *Vital Speeches,* Volume XVI, Number 15.

Enlist in the Battle for Men's Minds

Today's conflict is essentially a battle of minds. "Democracy cannot survive unless more and more of our people are educated to an understanding of what our American way of life is — how it works, how to strengthen it, how to protect it . . . . Therefore, now, at the fulltide of this dramatic century, let us rededicate ourselves to the great business of making democracy work; let us resolve to meet this mighty challenge by faithful citizenship and faithful stewardship—by being alert to change what is bad, by being determined to hold fast to what is good — so that the kind of government of which Lincoln spoke shall *not* perish from the earth."* To perpetuate our way of life we need leadership at every level — in high and humble places.

Speaking is an indispensable tool of leadership. It sharpens ability to think. In fact, clear speech comes *only* from clear thinking. To be a good leader you must have followers who esteem you because of your ability to fashion, champion, and defend a point of view.

You *can* learn to speak, and you *must* learn to speak! The president of one of our American colleges declares: "After spending so much time in directors' meetings listening to business men who can't speak, trying to put over ideas, I insist that every student must be able to talk clearly on his feet. What is the use of knowing all there is to know about a subject if you can't transmit your ideas to others quickly and convincingly?" There is much that is important to speak about today — freedom, citizenship, responsibility, world affairs, peace, understanding, and spirituality,

---

* *Ibid.*

to suggest but a few. All of us have so much at stake, we cannot afford to be neutral spirits — mute where truth cries out for the voices of free men.

To Be a Good Speaker, Be First of All a Good Man

Assume that you have learned to express yourself with some degree of skill: Is that all that you must do to become a good speaker? Quintilian stated that "according to my definition, no man can be a complete orator unless he is a *good* man: I therefore require that he should be not only all-accomplished in eloquence, but also possessed of every moral virtue." Demosthenes affirmed that "an orator is a *good* man speaking." Our own Ralph Waldo Emerson put *manliness* at the head of his list of qualifications for the speaker. What, then, are the most salient moral virtues the successful speaker *must* possess?

Speak the Simple Truth

Today the world needs men to speak the truth! What the writer means has been clearly expressed by Henry J. Taylor, noted news analyst, in these words: "Who says we are dumb and don't know what to do . . . ? If our judgments are weak, it may be because we have heard so much dishonest oratory that we have lost our powers of reason.

"For years we have been sold down the river . . . . So have millions elsewhere . . . . The world is facing a moral crisis just as much as it is facing a military or economic crisis.

"Essentially the problem is one of *integrity*. In a home, in a business, in a nation, integrity is what upholds all. It is this weakening of integrity that seems to me to be the greatest illness everywhere . . . . *The grand corruption of our age, in fact, is the inability of so many eminent human beings the world over to practice simple honesty and speak the simple truth.*"*

Glorify Intelligence

To discern the truth that lies buried as treasure within mountains of fact and fancy, you must dig honestly and intelligently. This requires sharp tools of the mind and the will of good intent. President Eliot of Harvard University summarized the process in four steps: "One, observing accurately; two, recording correctly; three, comparing, grouping, and *inferring justly*; and four, *expressing* the results."

Abbé Ernest Dimnet held that "Ideas are the roots of creation," and Confucius stated that "What is most needed for learning is a humble mind."

The vessel of knowledge must be intelligence. And the meaning of *intelligence* is embodied in the Latin roots of the word which translated are: *ability to choose between.* "It is the faculty by which one knows the beautiful from the ugly,

---

* "Let the Truth Be Heard," a radio address, number 288 in the series, *Your Land and Mine*, presented by General Motors.

the permanently valuable from the transient, the good from the bad, the better from the good . . . . One may be learned in philology or be a technically effective bacteriologist or be proficient in any one of a hundred kinds of specialized knowing, and yet remain unintelligent, incompetent to recognize comparative values, unable to make considered choices requisite for happiness or even for survival."*

Intelligence is nurtured by rigid self-discipline and wise self-direction. Henry van Dyke illuminated the meaning of true intelligence when he said:

> An intelligent man ought
> To think without confusion clearly;
> To love his fellow men sincerely,
> To act from honest motives purely,
> To trust in heaven and God securely!

Decry Sensationalism

Despite all our educational facilities too many of us are woefully careless. We gather fragments of information from tabloids and pulp magazines; we set our cultural standards according to the myths of Hollywood; we yield our government to the stratagems of professional politicians; and we blight our ideals of patriotism with tawdry display and shallow sentimentality. For many of us, religion has become a kind of mystic sensationalism wherein feeling is the sole criterion of good.

Our trouble has been diagnosed this way: "Picture magazines and tabloid newspapers place before millions, scenes and facts which violate every definition of humanity.

---

* Bernard Iddings Bell, "We Lack Leaders — Is Education at Fault?" in New York *Times Magazine*, January 18, 1948.

How common it is today to see upon the front page of some organ destined for a hundred thousand homes the agonized face of a child run over in the street, the dying expression of a woman crushed by a subway train, tableaus of execution, scenes of intense private grief. These are the obscenities. The rise of sensational journalism everywhere [including radio, cinema, theater, and television] testifies to man's . . . determination to enjoy the forbidden in the name of freedom.

"All reserve is being sacrificed to titillation. The extremes of passion and suffering are served up to enliven the breakfast table or to lighten the boredom of an evening at home. The area of privacy has been abandoned . . . ."*

In the sacred tradition of the Christian faith sensationalism is regarded as a sin. Two hundred years ago, John Wesley asked his mother: "What is sin?" Her reply might serve as a guide for all mankind today. She answered: "Would you judge of the lawfulness of pleasure, take this rule: Whatever weakens your reason, impairs the tenderness of your conscience, obscures your sense of God, takes off your relish for spiritual things — whatever increases the authority of the body over the mind — that is sin to you, however innocent it may seem in itself."

Live Not by Bread Alone

Are you one of those hard-pressed people who are slaves to life's machinery? Are music, art, books, and religion unimportant to you? Are you becoming a mere robot instead of a man?

---

* Richard M. Weaver, *Ideas Have Consequences*, p. 29. The University of Chicago Press, Chicago, Illinois, 1948. Reprinted by permission.

If you feel yourself engulfed by the materialism of our age, study the Scriptures, learn a lovely poem, read a good book, sing a beautiful song, pay court to the majesty of nature, and listen to the whisper of God! The truly great speakers have done precisely this. The dearth of moral giants among our leaders may be due to a creeping spiritual famine. General Omar Bradley warns of the hazards facing our generation. He says:

"Humanity is in danger of being trapped in this world by its moral adolescence. Our knowledge of science has clearly outstripped our capacity to control it.

"We have too many men of science; too few men of God.

"We have grasped the mystery of the atom and rejected the Sermon on the Mount.

"Man is stumbling blindly through a spiritual darkness while toying with the precarious secrets of life and death. The world has achieved brilliance without wisdom, power without conscience.

"Ours is a world of nuclear giants and ethical infants.

"We know more about war than we know about peace, more about killing than we know about living."*

The danger is an old one. It has lurked at every turn in civilization's upward road. When Rome was in her glory, Epictetus discerned: "In every feast, remember there are two guests to be entertained, the *body* and the *soul*; and that which you give the body you presently lose, but *what you give the soul remains forever.*"

---

* From Armistice Day speech at Boston, 1948.

The distinguished English historian, James Froude, wrote: "One lesson, and only one, history may be said to repeat with distinctness: That the world is built on moral foundations; that, in the long run, it is well with the good; in the long run, it is ill with the wicked . . . . The essence of true nobility is neglect of self. Let the thought of self pass in, and the beauty of a great action is gone, like the bloom from a soiled flower . . . . The beautiful character is the unselfish character."

Those who guide our youth today cry out: "The unpardonable sin for every human being is to have more knowledge than understanding; more power than love; to know more about the earth than the people who live in it; to invent quick means of travel to faraway places when one cannot grope one's way within one's own heart. For freedom is a dreadful thing unless it goes hand in hand with *responsibility*. Democracy among men is a specter, *except when the hearts of men are mature*."*

Listen to the wisdom of Louis Pasteur, as he spoke to the young men around him: "Blessed is the man who carries within him a God, an ideal, and who obeys it — ideal of art, ideal of science, ideal of the gospel virtues. Therein lie the springs of great thoughts and great actions."

Face Criticism Courageously

At twenty-five, while he was out hunting, Henry Fawcett was accidentally shot and blinded by his father's gun. His only remark was, "This shall make no difference." It didn't. He became Postmaster General of England. Beethoven never heard his *Ninth Symphony*, which he

---

* Extract from a report of American School Administrators.

composed after turning deaf. His last words were, "I shall hear in heaven." These were men of courage.

The speaker must also be a man of courage. He must serve his fellow men and stand for what he knows to be right. He must be able to endure censure, which, for many human beings, exceeds physical pain. Whether it is merited or not, criticism always follows in the wake of courageous action. Sir John Simon, British Chancellor of the Exchequer, hung a tapestry on his wall to help him face this fact. It read: "To Escape Criticism, Say Nothing, Do Nothing, Be Nothing."

Roland Hayes, the world-famous Negro tenor, was eating a meal in a dingy room because he was denied the privilege of entering the banquet hall. A white reporter found him there and exploded at such discrimination. Hayes smiled and explained: "My earliest teacher in voice, himself a Negro, told me that as an artist, a black artist, I would suffer terribly if I allowed the barbs to penetrate my soul; but if my heart was right, and my spirit divinely disciplined, then nobody in all the world would be able to hurt me. I know now that this is true. I try every moment of every day to live in such awareness of the presence of the divine that no bitterness can creep into my heart. Thus I have learned to be happy, and I have discovered that nobody in all the world can hurt me except myself." What a courageous attitude! Like Hayes, each of us should make criticism a part of our life's wealth. We should respect it instead of resent it, and analyze it for possible dividends.

Lincoln's attitude towards criticism is a model for the harassed person. He said: "If I tried to read, much less answer, all the criticisms made of me and all the attacks leveled against me, this office would be closed for all other business. *I do the best I know how, the very best I can.* I mean to keep on doing this, down to the very end. If the end brings me out all wrong, then ten angels swearing I had been right would make no difference. If the end brings me out all right, then what is said against me will not amount to anything." Perhaps Lincoln was guided by the wisdom of the Bible: "Faithful are the wounds of a friend; but the kisses of an enemy are deceitful."

Be Gallant with Tact

Of course, you should not be falsely courageous and speak ruthlessly. To substitute brazenness for courage is a weakness of character which may lead to irreparable offense. Tact is the better approach, for it expresses your desire to shield the other fellow from injury to his ego. Tact is the open eye and the quick ear to catch cues of danger to sensitive pride. It is a sincere regard for the welfare of others — a manifestation of modern gallantry.

Franklin's philosophy of tact is a worthy example: "The way to convince another is to state your case *moderately* and *accurately*. Then scratch your head, or shake it a little and say that is the way it seems to you, but that of course you may be mistaken about it; which causes your listener to receive what  you have to say, and as like as not, turn about and try to convince you of it, since you are in doubt. But if you go at him in a tone of positiveness and arrogance, you will only make an opponent of him."

Make Character Your Strength

To cultivate power of leadership, you should be the *good* man who speaks the simple truth. As presented in the foregoing pages, this *goodness* means that you glorify intelligence, that you are motivated by spiritual and moral values rather than by material and expedient ends, and that you speak with courage tempered by tact. The writer wishes to impress indelibly upon you — you who would learn to speak — that *character is your strength*. It is as true today as when Demosthenes spoke that the development of "every moral virtue," is required of the good speaker. It is not only part of the man, but *all* of him that must be perfected.

A GUIDE FOR SPEAKERS' LIBRARIES

Many excellent publications are quoted in this volume. Their content and nature are indicated in the excerpts. The footnotes cite title, author, and publisher. If you desire further information about any of the materials, inquire at your bookstore or public library. Additional works are listed here to help you in the preparation of your talks.

Books about Words

(How to pronounce words and achieve variety in their use.)

Roget's International Thesaurus. Thomas Y. Crowell Co., New York. 1964.

Webster's Dictionary of Synonyms. G. & C. Merriam Co., Springfield, Massachusetts. 1951.

Webster's New Seventh Collegiate Dictionary. G. & C. Merriam Co., Springfield, Massachusetts. 1965.

Bright Ideas Brilliantly Expressed

(Someone else may have put your idea into better words.)

Bartlett, John, *Familiar Quotations.* Little, Brown and Company, Boston. 1955. Collection of great quotations arranged according to author.

Edwards, Tryon, *The New Dictionary of Thought.* The Wise-Parslow Co., New York. 1960. Prose quotations on all subjects. Indexed and cross-indexed.

Mencken, H. L., *A New Dictionary of Quotations.* Alfred A. Knopf, New York. 1942. Contains unusual statements and is good reading in itself. No index.

Stevenson, Burton, *The Home Book of Quotations.* Dodd, Mead and Co., New York. 1964. Largest and most comprehensive book of its kind. Includes poetry and prose. Indexed and cross-indexed.

Stevenson, Burton, *The Home Book of Modern Verse.* Henry Holt and Co., New York. 1953. Two volumes. Most complete book of verse. Best index.

Jokes, Stories, and Wisecracks

Droke, Maxwell, *The Anthology of Anecdotes*. Droke House, Indianapolis. 1948. Tells how to use humor effectively and includes 295 meet-the-situation stories, etc.

Fuller, Edmund, *Thesaurus of Anecdotes*. Crown Publishers, New York. 1948.

Meiers, Mildred and Knapp, Jack, *Thesaurus of Humor*. Garden City Publishing Company, Inc., New York. 1948.

Prochnow, Herbert V., *The Public Speaker's Treasure Chest*. Harper & Brothers Publishers, New York. 1964.

Facts and Figures

Information Please Almanac. Doubleday and Co., New York. Published annually. On better paper, easier to use than *World Almanac*.

Vital Speeches of the Day. City News Publishing Co., 33 West 42nd St., New York. Published twice monthly. Contains complete texts of the best current speeches. Many quotations from this periodical are to be found in this book. Excellent source of information on contemporary America. Used widely in colleges.

Books about People

Current Biography. The H. W. Wilson Co., New York. Issued monthly with annual cumulations in one volume. Choice materials concerning people currently in the news.

The Reader's Encyclopedia. Edited by William Rose Benet. Thomas Y. Crowell Co., New York. 1965. Brief biographies of leading writers and references to literary characters and books.

Webster's Biographical Dictionary. G. & C. Merriam Co., Springfield, Massachusetts. 1964. Brief biographies of distinguished people of all countries and periods of time in one volume.

Consult *Readers' Guide to Periodical Literature* for help in finding material on specific subjects from magazines. To be found in most libraries. Indispensable. Remember to consult your local librarian and the encyclopedias.

SUGGESTED SPEECH ACTIVITIES

Read, converse, and fill your mind full. Then, let yourself go. Organize but do not memorize. Think on your feet and communicate. Keep talks brief — two or three minutes. Don't undertake too much at first or become impatient if your progress seems slow to you.

Activities to Make You Feel at Home before an Audience

1. Get acquainted. Tell the group who you are, your name and how to remember it, where you work and what you do. Why you want to learn to speak. About your hobbies or other human interest facts about yourself. Have fun.

2. Present in detail one single interesting experience. Your most exciting trip. Your most embarrassing situation or the funniest. A fire or accident you saw. Your first job. How you earned your first dollar. Your greatest mistake. If you had your life to live over.

3. Use bodily action. Demonstrate first lessons in golf, tennis, etc., using clubs and racket. First aid to the injured. Parlor tricks. Strokes in swimming. How to tip your hat to the ladies. Good and bad table manners. Show scrapbooks, keepsakes, curios, and mechanical devices. Tell where you got them, what they mean to you, and how they work.

4. Pantomime. Use no words in this exercise: Act out a simple story. Show how you shave, make-up, drive, fish, hunt, bowl, change a tire, build something, dress, hitchhike, escort a date, or portray some other action idea.

5. Argue against your pet peeve. Select a subject about which you really get excited — one that makes you boil or want to fight. Be specific: give plenty of details and examples. Talk about the rude policeman who gave you a ticket. What happened when you lent money to a friend. That raw deal. The used car that turned out to be a "lemon." How you were insulted. Someone at work who annoys you. How you hate war, race prejudice, cruelty to dumb animals.

6. Attract attention. Two students should occupy opposite ends of the platform and speak to the group on entirely different subjects at the same time. The speakers must ignore each other but vie with each other for the listeners' attention. Use topics like those listed in number five above. Don't scream, but use an abundance of animation and action. Limit speaking time to one minute.

7. Overcome hecklers. Speak for or against more than two terms for the President of the United States, married women in industry, strikes, uniform marriage and divorce laws, the outlawing of the atomic bomb, yellow journalism, television, prohibition, advertising, radio commercials, etc. Listeners will interrupt the speaker with such questions as, "What do you mean?" "Who says so?" "Explain the point more in detail!" "How do you know?" The audience should put the speaker through the fire, loosen him up, but should not carry the heckling too far. If the speaker is talking with vitality, let up on the heckling. The speaker must keep his head, prevent hecklers from stopping his speaking, and frame answers to silence them. He must be aggressive and never permit the meeting to pass from his control.

8. Emote! Select a nursery rhyme like "Tom, Tom, the Piper's Son," "Old Mother Hubbard," or "Mary Had a Little Lamb" for rendition in small groups of six or eight. See which group can deliver a rhyme with maximum animation, anger, unexpressiveness, sadness, indignation, or laughter. Whisper the rhyme, shout it, dramatize it, shed tears over it.

Activities to Help You Find and Share Material

1. Talk about a book similar to those listed on pages 262-63. Describe what's in it and quote a line or two. Highlight the human interest material. Arouse the group to wish to own it.

2. Choose a human interest article from a magazine like *Reader's Digest, Time,* or *Harper's* and tell why the article appeals to you. Make your discussion alive and compelling.

3. Select a challenging editorial from a newspaper or periodical. Quote a few statements and agree or disagree.

4. Build a talk around a visit to a minister, lawyer, doctor, or mortician. Discuss the qualifications for his profession. Take a tour through a poultry plant, slaughterhouse, mill, cannery, or candy factory and tell your group about the main features of the industry.

5. Build a round-table discussion on a current problem: How to improve our city, family life, government, etc. Use materials and techniques illustrated on pages 149-159.

6. Find some stories, quotations, and verses similar to those indicated on page 272 and build a talk around them.

7. Tell one of Aesop's fables and develop a point around the moral: "The race is not always to the swift." "Pride goes before a fall." "In unity is strength." Use additional facts and examples in support of the idea.

Activities to Help You Organize Your Ideas

Using examples, stories, facts, and other items, build a talk similar to "Emerson Is Right," pages 137-38, "Don't Die on Third," pages 132-35. Also employ the topical order, point follows proof, and proof follows point, and the other methods outlined in Chapter XI. Study and prepare introductions and conclusions like those in Chapter XIV.

Under the wise guidance of a teacher, these activities can be expanded and adapted to meet your needs.

ARE YOU READY TO SPEAK?
(Check this questionnaire.)

I. HAVE I INVESTIGATED THE OCCASION?
    A. What is its purpose?
    B. What is taking place?
    C. What else is on the program?

II. HAVE I DETERMINED UNDER WHAT PHYSICAL CONDITIONS I SPEAK?
    A. Outdoors or indoors?
    B. Before a microphone?
    C. Size of auditorium?
    D. Are light, heating, and ventilation adequate?

III. HAVE I EXAMINED MY OWN ATTITUDES AND FEELINGS?
    A. Do I know my subject thoroughly?

B. Am I genuinely interested in it?

C. Am I eager to get my message over?

D. Will I have an enjoyable time presenting it?

E. Have I used imagination and creative thought in preparation?

F. Has my talk developed from my own experience, investigation, reading, and conversation?

IV. HAVE I ANALYZED THE AUDIENCE?

A. How large will it be?

B. What is the predominant age?

C. Of what sex will it be composed?

D. What is its educational background:
   1. Schooling and training?
   2. Experience?

E. What is its religious interest?

F. What are its occupation and income:
   1. Manual, intellectual, professional, or managerial?

G. What are its primary interests?
   1. What do my listeners want most?
   2. How are these wants related to my subject?

H. Is it friendly, indifferent, or hostile:
   1. Toward me?
   2. Toward my subject?
   3. Toward my speech purpose?

I. How much does it know about the subject?

V. HAVE I CAREFULLY PREPARED MY SUBJECT?

A. What is my general purpose?

B. What is my specific purpose?
   1. Have I one big point?
   2. Is it briefly and clearly formulated?
   3. Does it fit the audience, occasion, and *time limits*?
   4. Is it developed through the use of speech details, facts, and illustrations?
   5. Does my talk have an effective introduction and conclusion?
   6. Does my speech have well-planned transitions and climaxes?
   7. Have I checked my language and pronunciation?
   8. Have I practiced to attain pleasing voice and expressive gestures?

Part of your own development as a speaker is achieved in listening intelligently to other speakers. This questionnaire will be valuable in helping you analyze their talks.

INDEX

INDEX

(Continued)

INDEX

(Continued)

INDEX

(Continued)

SELECTED STORIES AND QUOTATIONS
from
YOU CAN LEARN TO SPEAK !

(Add others of your own choice.)

SUBJECT	PAGE	SUBJECT	PAGE
....		....	
....		....	
....		....	
....		....	
....		....	
....		....	
....		....	
....		....	
....		....